Turn Eye Appeal into Buy Appeal:

How to easily transform your marketing pieces into dazzling, persuasive sales tools!

Karen Saunders

MacGraphics
services

*Where your ideas
become distinctive designs*

Turn Eye Appeal into Buy Appeal

How to Easily Transform Your Marketing Pieces into Dazzling, Persuasive Sales Tools!

By Karen Saunders

Published by:
MacGraphics Services
Aurora, Colorado, USA

All rights reserved for entire book. Reproduction or translation of any part of this work by any means without permission of the publisher is unlawful.

This publication is designed to provide accurate and authoritative information regarding the subject matter. The author/publisher does not assume any responsibility for errors, omissions, or contrary interpretation of the subject matter herein. The author/publisher cannot be held liable for any success or failure of the readers' businesses that is directly or indirectly related to the purchase and use of the information herein.

Copyright © 2006 by Karen Saunders of MacGraphics Services
10-Digit ISBN: 0-9785371-3-0
13-Digit ISBN: 978-0-9785371-3-5
Printed in the United States of America
Library of Congress Control Number: 2006939863

The cover, interior layout, and all graphics in this guide were done by MacGraphics Services except for the following items: the ICF logo, NSA logo, Doug Butler Enterprises, Inc. logo, Lin McNeil's first book, and Kendall SummerHawk's website. Clip art and stock photos are from various sources. A special thanks to Joyce M. Turley for drawing the "eye" icon.

Editing by Barbara McNichol, Barbara McNichol Editorial

Contact Information:
Toll-Free Phone: 888-796-7300
Website: www.macgraphics.net

About the Author

Karen Saunders founded MacGraphics Services in 1990. This graphic design firm in Aurora, Colorado, helps business owners present themselves and their services effectively in the marketplace through well-designed pieces. They include ads, logos, flyers, book covers and interiors, corporate identity, audio and video packaging, and much more. Karen has designed the covers of 21 books that have become best-sellers or won awards, including the 2005 *Writer's Digest* "Grand Prize" winner for the best self-published book in America.

Karen earned a Bachelor of Fine Arts degree in graphic design from Western Michigan University in 1982. A self-taught computer graphic designer, she has been production manager for Cimarron Productions and Genigraphics, both computer graphics and multimedia firms. For several years, she taught desktop publishing classes at Community College of Denver, University of Colorado at Boulder, and Rocky Mountain College of Art and Design. She served Colorado Independent Publishers Association (CIPA) as a board member, program director, and wrote the "Desktop Coach" column for CIPA's newsletter for three years.

Karen's articles on desktop publishing have appeared in *The Boulder County Business Report, Broker Agent News, Business Scene, Building Savvy, Insurance Insight, Fabricare, SPAN Connection* (Small Publishers Association of North America), and *Publishers Marketing Association (PMA) Newsletter.* She has also given presentations for Mark Victor Hansen's Mega Marketing Magic event, Sales Professionals International, CIPA, and Zonta International.

Visit Karen's website at **www.macgraphics.net** for samples of her work and free articles on desktop publishing.

Karen won a 2006 APEX Award for Publication Excellence for the ebook version of this guide. The award was based on excellence in graphic design, editorial content and in achieving overall communications effectiveness and excellence.

A Note From the Author

Perhaps this is the first time you've sat down at your computer to design a marketing piece, announce a product, or create a sales flyer. Or you're just starting to add graphic elements to the words you've put on paper. Or you're working with a designer and want to understand the process and terminology better. Or you've been putting together your own marketing pieces for a while—you just want insights on how to do it better! With this guide for illustrators, authors, administrative assistants, and business owners who design and produce their own books and marketing pieces, you've got the right tool at your fingertips.

Congratulations for learning how to add more eye appeal to your designs and more sales appeal to your marketing pieces.

To your success,

Karen Saunders

Karen Saunders
Author/designer

Contents

Good Marketing Requires Good Design 7
    10 Questions to Answer Before Designing
        Your Next Project 8
    5-Step Workflow for Designing and
        Producing Your Printed Piece 10

Make Visual Elements Memorable 13
    Branding: An Umbrella Concept You Can't Ignore 14
    What Makes a Good Logo Design? 16
    Checklist for Designing a Successful Logo 18
    Tagging the Best Tag Line for Your Business 19
    Building a Better Business Card 21
    Why Maintain a Consistent Visual Identity? 23

Writing Persuasive Content And Making It Flow 27
    Think in the Prospect's Perspective 28
    Capturing Customers with Persuasive Words.............30
    Marketing Writing That Gets Read 33
    How to Improve Your Proofreading Skills................36

The Best Typography For Design And Readability 39
    Start with the ABCs 40
    Legibility and Readability of Fonts 41
    Choosing Fonts 42
    How to Match Your Font to Your Message 43
    Setting the Tone of Your Text
        with Kerning, Tracking, and Leading..............................44
    9 Typesetting Tricks That Design Pros Use 48
    Shopping for Types of Fonts...............................51

Laying Out Your Pages With Style 53
    6 Elements that Make Your Design Effective 54
    The Magic of Working with Grids........................56
    Working with Images to Enhance Your Layout..................58
    Jazz Up Your Layouts with Pull Quotes 60
    A Checklist of Features that Add Eye Appeal 62

Design Solutions For Specific Projects 65
- 10 Questions to Answer Before Designing Your Flyer..........66
- What Makes a Flyer A "Must-Have" Marketing Tool?..........67
- A Client-Capturing Website Builds Your Brand *and* Your Bottom Line 70
- Creating Presentations That Wow Audiences......................72
- Tips for Designing Book Covers and Inside Pages 76

Working With Digital Imagery..81
- Learning to Work with Digital Photos................................82
- What to Consider When Buying a Scanner 86
- How to Scan Photos at the Correct Resolution..................88

The Role Of Color In Your Design 91
- How Color Can Add "Zing" to Your Design......................92
- Easy Ways to Select Harmonious Colors 94
- Unlocking the Symbolic Meaning of Color 96
- RGB and CMYK—Colorful but Different........................98
- Making Monitor Colors Match Your Printed Piece 100

Getting Graphics Files Ready To Print 103
- Proper File Formats for Internet and Print.......................104
- The Versatility of PDF Files...106
- Checklist for Making Your Files Print-Ready...................108

Answers To Your Printing Questions................................. 111
- What Should You Consider When Choosing a Printer?.....112
- What's the Difference Between a Digital and Offset Printer?...114
- How Can You Save Money on Color Printing?................116
- How Can You Maximize Two-Color Printing? 118
- What Paper Works Best? 120
- What Special Effects Will Add Flair to Your Print Job?......124
- What Kind of Folding Do You Need?..............................126
- What are Your Options for Binding? 127

Resources...131

What Comes Next 133

Good Marketing Requires Good Design

Why should you care about *Good Design* when you put your company's materials out into the world?

In two words, *Good Marketing*.

For *Good Marketing* that catches attention and delivers the intended message (doesn't every businessperson want that?), step up your ability to weave *Good Design* into every marketing piece. When you do, you'll reinforce your branding strategy, be more "in charge" of quality, and leave a lasting impression with your prospects and clients.

With *Good Marketing* in mind, this first section provides a checklist of questions and an overview of the design and production process.

In this section, you'll learn about:

- **10 questions to answer before designing your next project**
- **5-step workflow for designing and producing your printed piece**

10 Questions To Answer Before Designing Your Next Project

You're ready to begin—or think you are. But first, get centered and start asking the right questions.

Here are the questions I ask myself and my clients *before* any design project begins. Answer them for your upcoming project; they'll help you get organized and make life easier once you do get going.

1. What is the purpose of your project: to entertain, inform, persuade? Keep your marketing purpose in mind when you write the text, gather visuals to support the text, and set up your design.

2. Who is your intended target audience? Identifying your audience helps you to grab their interest by choosing the best style of graphics, writing, colors, and more.

3. What look do you want your final product to have and how will you design it? Working through the sections in this guide will definitely help you answer this one! You want to address how to deal with typography, content, color, photography, and more.

4. What is your graphics theme? Develop a theme and stick with it. Your text, fonts, and graphics should all build and support the theme you've selected. The graphics theme for Wells Fargo bank, for example, is the stagecoach.

5. What graphic information will you include? Fill in any gaps you have in your content with illustrations, photos, tables, quotes, and other graphic elements. When you gather these elements first, you'll have a visual sense of how much space they will take up as you lay out your design.

Good Marketing Requires Good Design

6. How will your project be produced? Again, this guide will help you answer that question. In particular, make sure you thoroughly read about preparing your files for the printer. (See Getting Graphics Files Ready To Print.)

7. Have you talked with your printer about print specifications for this project? It is important to determine trim size (final size of a printed piece), binding, bleeds (the area of a graphic or photo that extends beyond the edge of the trimmed sheet), number of inks, choice of spot inks or process inks, folds and scores (creasing paper mechanically so it will fold more easily), paper stock, and more before you even begin your design. Use the section dedicated to printing as your online consultant. (See Answers To Your Printing Questions.)

8. What postal regulations may affect your design? If your piece will be mailed, check with the post office for regulations regarding labeling, folding, size restrictions, the weight of the paper to use, proper positioning, and exact wording of postal information on the mailer you're designing. For details, read "Designing Letter and Reply Mail" (Publication 25) on the USPS web site: http://pe.usps.gov/text/pub25/pub25.htm

9. What is your schedule? Work backward and determine a realistic timetable for all elements of your project: distributing, labeling, binding, printing, proofreading, designing, editing, writing, and planning.

10. What is the cost for each step of the process in your budget? Create a budget, then take time to shop around for the best prices—combined with quality and turnaround time—that come within your budget.

By answering these questions, you will be better prepared for the five steps in the production process—the natural workflow for your project.

5-Step Workflow for Designing and Producing Your Printed Piece

Now that you've got an overview of what's needed from the previous 10 questions, your next job is to make the design process go smoothly by following these five steps.

Step 1 — Organize, Plan, Budget

First, set the budget and deadline for your project. Your budget includes all or some of the following: writing, designing, editing, proofreading, illustrations, photography or stock imagery, choosing the right paper, printing, folding, binding, labeling, and distributing.

Everything that goes into making the printed piece comes under the term "production." To determine various production deadlines, start with the date you want customers to receive your piece and work backward. Leave enough time for the elements noted above. Set deadlines for completing each of these functions.

Step 2 — Concept, Design, Text and Images

Clearly identify your target audience and determine what you want to achieve with your printed piece (e.g., increase your marketing exposure, establish your corporate identity, launch an advertising campaign, etc.).

Outline a "design brief" that clarifies your concepts, goals, and budget for the project. This will help you (or your designer) tailor the design, typography, graphics, and color to your targeted audience. Thinking through these elements of the concept early will also help you stay within your budget. Do black and white "thumbnail" sketches by hand (which are small—about 2" x 2" drawings) of your ideas on paper.

Prepare your text in a word processing program or hire a writer to compose text and headlines to fit the space you need. (See Writing Persuasive Content And Making It Flow section for writing and proofreading tips.) It's best to collaborate closely with the writer at this "brainstorming" stage to develop a theme and determine the

A "thumbnail" sketch of an ad. Horizontal lines indicate text.

Good Marketing Requires Good Design

right amount of text and graphics needed. If you write the copy yourself, I highly recommend hiring an editor to perfect the language and ensure it's easy to understand.

Use professional drawing programs such as Corel Draw, Adobe Illustrator or Macromedia Freehand to do your graphics. Then, use photo-editing software such as Adobe Elements or Adobe Photoshop to touch up and crop your scans and photos. Determine what file formats and resolution your graphics and scans should be to produce this project. Don't hesitate to consult with a designer or printer to get this right! (See How to Scan Photos at the Correct Resolution and Proper File Formats for Internet and Print.)

Step 3 — Page Layout

Once you select a general direction for your project, use a professional page layout program such as Adobe InDesign or Quark Xpress to design your color "comps." (This means compiling the text and graphics into one document.) Use "grids" to help with the positioning and alignment of text and graphics. (See The Magic of Working with Grids.) Then print your comps as laser prints or low-resolution color PDFs. (See The Versatility of PDF Files.)

If you have a multiple page project such as a newsletter, you should design style sheets for reoccurring type treatments. (Setting up style sheets lets you automatically format your text, subheads, headlines, etc.) Using style sheets saves a lot of time throughout the production process. You can have a professional designer set them up for you.

Step 4 — Editing and Proofing

Proofread, proofread, proofread! Hire an editor and/or proofreader for assurance that written mistakes on the piece get noticed and fixed. Be sure to dial all the phone and fax numbers printed on your layout and go to all the websites to confirm that the stated website locations are correct. At the same time, make sure your design aligns well with the words, that the correct captions appear under the illustrations and photographs, and so on.

At this stage, it is best to output high-resolution digital color proofs so you can see a close color reproduction of your piece. Alternatively, you could proofread the pages from a set of black and white or color laser prints. Be sure to review the entire layout before you prepare the files for the printer.

The Design and Production Workflow

- Planning Budgeting
- Concept Design
- Writing Editing / Images: Illustrations Scans Photos
- Page Layout
- Minor Editing Proofreading
- Pre-Press Proofs
- Printing Binding
- Distribution

11

Step 5 — Pre-Press, Approvals, and Printing

Perform a pre-flight checklist (see Checklist for Making Your Graphics Print-Ready), or convert your file to the PDF format to ensure that all graphics and fonts are included in the files sent to the printer. Beware: Skipping this step can lead to delays at the printing stage.

Some printers require a completed "file prep form" to ensure files are submitted properly. For traditionally printed color pieces, the printer prepares a color "matchprint" proof. Alternatively, your printer may give you digital color or black and white proof prints. It's important to carefully review these proofs for accuracy in matching the colors before printing.

For traditionally printed one or two color jobs, you'll review blueline proofs, which are contact prints of the film negatives. Made of light-sensitive, off-white material, bluelines show your layout printed in light-blue and medium-blue colors. From these bluelines, you can read the type and distinguish the color breaks (division of colors). Pay careful attention to these bluelines. This is your last opportunity to review your piece before it gets printed. Remember, any changes made at this point are very costly. Please note, most printers are discontinuing matchprints and bluelines, and are now using digital proofs.

Once you sign off on these proofs, you may want to do a press check, which takes place at your printer's facility while your project runs on the press. At this stage, you verify that the colors and other details are correct before the entire quantity is printed. During the press check process, you get a preview of your finished piece and come away with a sample hot off the press!

Make Visual Elements Memorable

This section begins by reviewing an overreaching marketing concept called branding. From branding stems myriad elements, but this guide focuses on the key visual elements in the branding mix—visual identity, logo, and tag line—then applies these elements to build a better business card.

In this section, you'll learn more about:

- **Branding: An umbrella concept you can't ignore**
- **What makes a good logo design?**
- **Checklist for designing a successful logo**
- **Tagging the best tag line for your business**
- **Building a better business card**
- **Why maintain a consistent visual identity?**

Branding: An Umbrella Concept You Can't Ignore

Branding: It's not only among the hottest marketing concepts that has surfaced in the last decade, but its overarching reach touches every aspect of a company.

Think of branding as *predefining what a company is all about in the minds of its clients*. It encompasses all the factors that make up both the recognition and interaction parts of doing business with that company.

According to branding expert Dick Bruso, in its broadest sense, branding strategically sets up a successful "umbrella" experience for clients and gives your company a strong foundation. This concept includes visual identity elements such as logos and graphics, but it also takes into account product mix, pricing, ambience, promotions, and much more.

Prime Example: Starbucks

Want an example of branding? Walk no farther than your nearest Starbucks. With its highly successful branding strategy, this coffee chain has created distinctive stores, an easily recognized logo and graphic identity, plus a total experience that cuts across language and cultural barriers. Every store features product, décor, and signage consistencies so you can "read its shorthand" and quickly understand what the company delivers.

If you've experienced having a drink at one Starbucks, chances are you'll have a similar experience at another. Few elements vary from store to store; you likely know most of the items on its menu before you ever walk in. That consistency leads to instant recognition and the promise of quality in marketplaces all over. Starbucks knows people are more likely to choose a coffee shop they recognize over an unknown competitor across the street. Multiply that experience by all the ways Starbucks reaches its millions of customers, and it demonstrates what mega-branding can do.

From a businessperson's perspective, a well-executed branding process brings recognition, reputation building, and ultimately sales, together in the minds of its targeted clients. When branding is done well, it can make a client's decision to buy go quickly and easily. People want to do business with people they know and like—and the branding process aims to portray a company as both knowable and likeable.

Perception of Value

How you brand your own company separates it from its competitors. You use branding to set high standards and give you a professional stature—an image of quality. It takes into account being a consistent, positive performer and delivering on what you promise. You want people to do business with you based on the "buzz" your branding has built. It comes down to the marketplace perception of your value. Ideally, that perception aligns with your intentions!

As you produce your marketing pieces, all the elements of your visual identity contribute to your entire branding process. Make them congruent with the complete branding picture you want to paint. Then, simply by seeing your logo, clients will attribute to your company the values you strive to achieve.

Heard Above The Noise™

Dick Bruso, founder of Heard Above The Noise™ asks these key questions for anyone wanting to build a successful brand. "What does your brand stand for? What absolutely sets you apart in everything you do, say, or communicate in any form? And what needs are you meeting, which will be highly valued by your target market(s) or specific niche?"

Dick believes we need to brand ourselves based upon who we are, what we stand for, and the ultimate value we bring to those we serve. By applying the umbrella concept to branding you are certain to be "heard above the noise" in today's crowded marketplace.

Branding expert Dick Bruso can be reached at 303-841-5122, or dickbruso@heardabove.com. His web site is www.heardabove.com.

What Makes a Good Logo Design?

Integrate abstract shapes into letters

Use color gradients

Use distinctive symbols and colors

Your logo is a graphic element that's designed to visually represent your company. Its purpose is to communicate at a glance your company's essence: what it does and what it stands for. As an integral part of your company's corporate identity and branding strategy, you should plan to use your logo with consistency for many years.

Don't be fooled; it's not easy to create a design that looks simple. In fact, the best logo designs are sophisticated in their simplicity. They combine and refine symbols, colors, and typography as well as negative and positive space into a compact unit.

What happens when you create a logo (or hire a designer to do it)? You'll develop several "comps" or preliminary design compositions. Then you'll select and analyze your final choices and perfect the one that represents you and your company best.

Merging Symbols and Letters

As you can see from the examples, logos are often the result of a symbiotic merging of a symbol with one or more letters in your company's name.

A good logo has a strong, balanced image with no little extras that clutter its look. A logo that's bold will be easier to see at a glance and works better than one that has thin, delicate lines or fonts.

Take time to ensure that all graphic imagery is streamlined and looks appropriate for your business. Your company name and the logo itself should work together as a unit. As you strive to achieve a distinctive look, avoid trendy fonts and extremely tall or wide logos.

Looks Good in Color and B&W

Although color logos are most common, make sure your logo design also looks good in black and white. How can you tell? Simply print it out on a black and white laser printer. Someday you'll want to use black and white version of your logo on a check, fax, or newspaper ad. You could use a screen (gray halftone) as an easy substitute to represent one of the colors in a black and white document.

Make Visual Elements Memorable

Reverse out areas to create positive and negative space

Play with double meaning on symbols

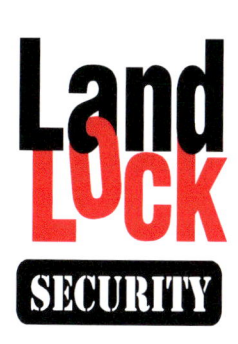

Interweave or overlap letters; use symbolic meaning of color

Choose an appropriate spot color and record its ink formula and/or number for future printing jobs. If your 2- or 3-color logo is printed in a full color publication (e.g., for use in a magazine ad), it may have to be converted to 4-color process inks. Getting a close match may not always be possible; check a spot-color-to-process-color conversion swatch book first.

You may be tempted to design a full-color logo, especially for use on your website, but beware that it will be expensive to print. Because full-color logos must be printed in 4-color process inks, you'll find it's much more economical to print your stationery pieces (e.g., letterhead, business cards, envelopes, etc.) in one, two, or three colors.

Converting into a Graphic

Once you have a logo designed, your next step is to convert all the text on the logo using "outlines" or "paths" (commands in the design software program). This converts your text into a "graphic"; you can't go back and alter your text after doing this. It's now a picture, not text made of letters. By doing that, you don't need to include separate fonts when transporting your logo to different computers, service providers, or printers. In fact, it's wise to convert your logo into the various file formats appropriate for the Internet, presentations, inkjet and laser printers, and offset printing. (See Proper File Formats for Internet and Print.)

Protecting Your Logo Design

You can register your logo as a trademark, although this can be a costly and time-consuming process. Contact a trademark attorney about options available.

Checklist for Designing a Successful Logo

A business logo that's strong and creative is comprised of these important design characteristics:

1. Simple, yet sophisticated
2. Distinctive, bold, and graphic (no thin lines)
3. Not extremely tall or wide
4. Not trendy or old-fashioned
5. Looks in balance
6. Works well in all sizes
7. Works well in color or black and white
8. Graphic element and name work together as a unit
9. Communicates your business clearly
10. Uses graphics and fonts appropriate for your business

LOEFFLER & ASSOCIATES
Mix free form art and graphics

SUMMIT Software Systems, Inc.
Contrast size and weight of fonts

CASTLE CREEK Enterprises
Change letters into symbols

*Visit **www.macgraphics.net** to see more sample logos*

Tagging the Best Tag Line for Your Business

Just as important as having a strong logo, you should also have a strong "tag line." The best tag line helps "brand" your business by succinctly describing who you are and what you can do for your clients. It should appear with your logo on your business cards, stationery, ads, website, and any other marketing pieces.

Most often, a tag line hugs a logo and trips easily off the tongue. (Think of Nike's *Just Do It* tag line or this common one: *We bring ideas to light!* Do you know which company it belongs to?)

Search the Internet and you'll discover lots of entrepreneurs describing their businesses through their tag lines. I suggest you find favorite examples before you write yours. Play with dozens of words and phrases. Put together crazy combinations, just for the fun of it. Ask a dozen trusted friends which tag lines from your list of favorites attract them and which don't.

Picking Your Tag Line

Yes, it's largely a trial-and-error process but good tag lines meet a number of criteria that will help you in your marketing.

- Can every word in your tag line be pronounced easily and spelled accurately (unless you intentionally misspell a word or two for effect)?

- Does yours sound too close to familiar tag lines already being used?

- Does it stand out with distinction like a color ad in a newspaper or blend in with all the gray newsprint?

- Is it so long-winded that people have to take a breath in the middle of saying it?

- Can it be easily remembered and quickly repeated?

- Does the message in the tag line suit what you sell or are you stretching the truth just a tad?

- Most important, does it imply a promise that you can't deliver on—like a carpet-cleaning company guaranteeing that carpets will stay clean for two years?

Here are examples of great tag lines.

The Julian Group
The Speaker Whose Message Means Business

Double "O" Good Alpacas
Where Trust and Quality Make a Difference

Barbara McNichol Editorial
Open Doors to Your Dreams through the Written Word

MacGraphics services

Where your ideas become distinctive designs

Building a Better Business Card

An example of amateurish business card design

When you distribute business cards at meetings and networking functions, your card may be the only item prospective clients will see. Having a good logo design and a clean layout leaves them with a favorable first impression that you're a credible professional businessperson.

Your business card is also part of your stationery system. A good system includes well-coordinated cards, letterhead, envelopes, and possibly mailing labels. You should use a grid to align your logo, tag line, and contact information in the same manner on all pieces of your stationery package. (For an explanation of using grids, go to The Magic of Working with Grids.)

Here's what to do and what to avoid:

Look at the sample business card on the top left as an example of what you should avoid doing. Note these points:

- There is no system of alignment. Text and graphics are pasted everywhere, filling up all the white space. Because of that, there is no focal point or central place that draws a reader's eye.

- The "highlight" color (red) is used so frequently that it simply doesn't stand out against the background.

- The color red may grab attention, but it has no symbolic meaning when applied to lawn care. Green would be a better choice.

- Rather than using six (!) different fonts, limit your selection to two fonts and their families. (A type family usually includes the **bold,** *italic,* and ***bold-italic*** versions of the font. Some fonts have extended families with condensed, ultra, black, etc.)

- Because the graphic elements are too detailed, they run together during the print process and look "muddy" (certainly not professional).

Turn Eye Appeal into Buy Appeal

The three examples on this page indicate good design choices compared with the one on the previous page that's poorly designed. Good design includes these elements:

- You can see an obvious grid as well as an alignment of objects and text with each other.

- Plenty of white space is apparent, giving the possibility for a definite focal point.

- Text is limited to two fonts rather than six.

- Text is smaller, more compact, and more professional looking.

This well-designed, conventional 2-color card uses one spot color plus black ink.

This well-designed card uses one spot color and black ink with a grayscale photo.

This dynamic full-color card uses 4-color process inks. The photo is cut out of its background and bleeds off the bottom of the card for maximum impact. (Note: Some printing companies now offer low prices on full-color business cards, although full-color letterheads and envelopes are still expensive.) If you use letterhead and envelopes infrequently, you might choose to print them only as you need them on your desktop color printer. The quality may not be as high as with offset printing, but it will likely serve your needs at a much lower cost.

Why Maintain a Consistent Visual Identity?

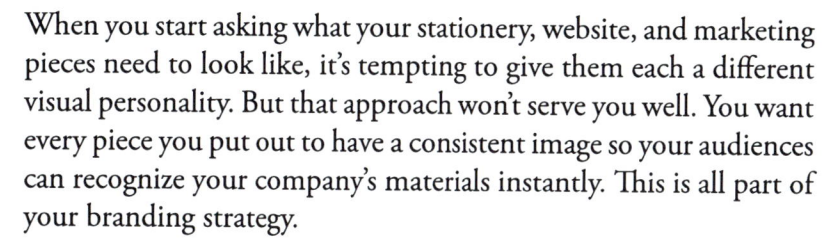

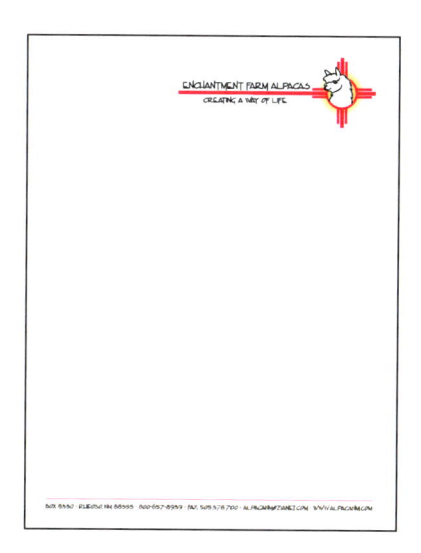

When you start asking what your stationery, website, and marketing pieces need to look like, it's tempting to give them each a different visual personality. But that approach won't serve you well. You want every piece you put out to have a consistent image so your audiences can recognize your company's materials instantly. This is all part of your branding strategy.

You'll notice how big corporations take that mandate seriously. Experts know that setting up and maintaining a specific visual image through logos, fonts, and layout give their companies credibility and stability in their markets. That principle holds true for every business, no matter how small or large it might be.

For Your Corporate Identity

I suggest you design a clean, professional-looking logo that represents the vision and essence of your company. Be prepared to use this identifying mark for a long time. You can protect the integrity of your corporate identity by making sure the color, fonts, and positioning of your logo are exactly the same on all materials. Always keep a copy of your logo file handy on your hard drive.

Your logo, business card, letterhead, and #10 envelope are the core pieces of a corporate identity package. You may choose to add labels, note cards, and stickers to fill out your package.

A typical stationery package consists of a business card, letterhead, and #10 envelope. Note, these samples are not at the same scale.

For Your Advertising and Marketing Campaigns

Create design features that establish a distinct identity for every campaign you do and all the materials that go with it. In addition to having your company's logo and colors appear on all printed pieces, make sure every element related to the campaign—all banners, giveaway items, promotional ads, etc.—carry through the graphic theme of the campaign itself. Give your event a style of its own while making sure it's easily associated with your company. (See examples on the following page.)

Develop Your Own Graphics Standards Manual

How do you keep track of all these design elements? Corporations develop a complex graphics standards manual to spell out the exact requirements of the identity that's been designed. Developing your own simple version of a manual standardizes the quality and look of everything you produce: in-house forms, slide presentations, newsletters, and so on. By following it, you'll see how consistent quality control saves time and money while enhancing communication and supporting your brand.

You may feel that having to adhere to a standard format puts a damper on your style. In fact, the opposite is true. You'll find it frees you to put new elements into a well-designed format and, because of that, it increases the clarity and effectiveness of each piece, every time.

The design of this trade journal ad is consistent with the ranch's corporate identity materials.

Make Visual Elements Memorable

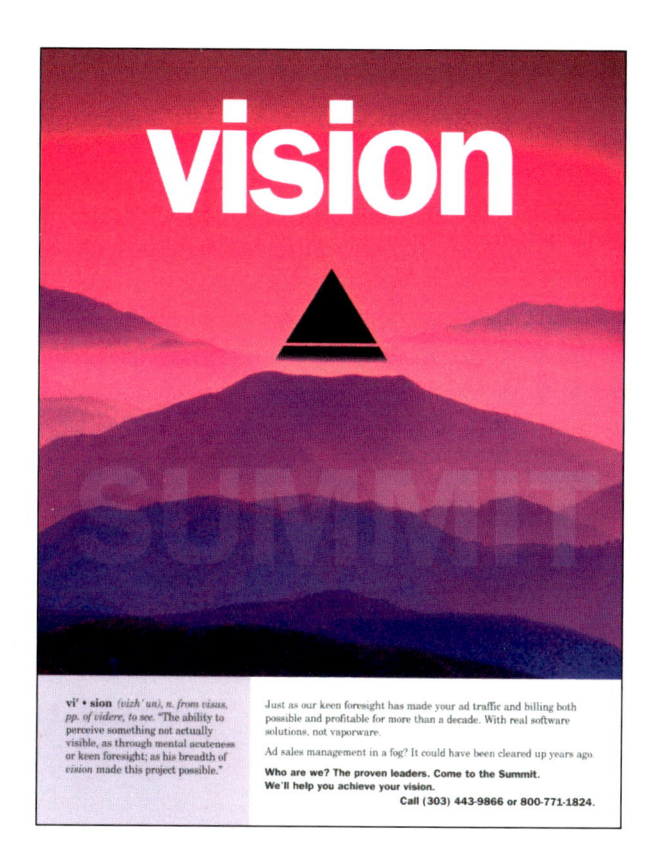

The graphics in this advertising campaign for Summit Software Systems, Inc. use a mountain-climbing theme throughout the three-part magazine ad series.

The company's new logo was graphically revealed over the course of the ads, and finally became fully visible in this double-page spread.

25

Turn Eye Appeal into Buy Appeal

The tri-fold continued the mountain-climbing theme with climbing tools, computer paper shaped like mountain peaks, and the same photos that were used in the ads.

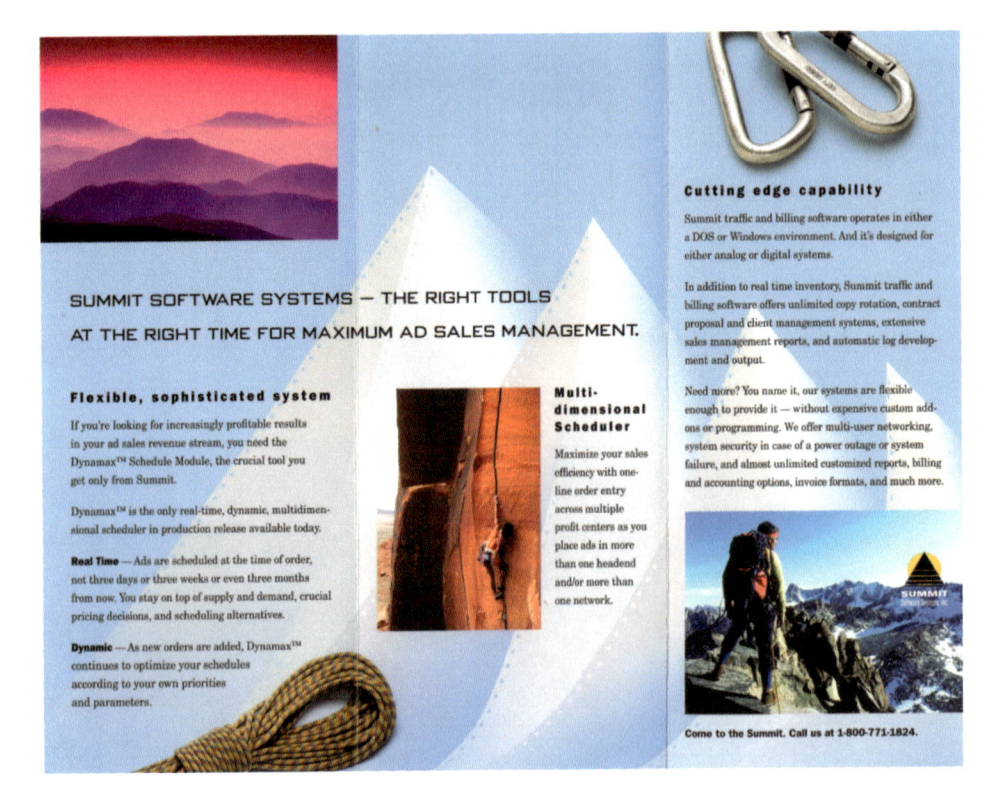

Writing Persuasive Content And Making It Flow

Although the focus of this guide is design, you can't ignore the need to write copy that enhances the design and vice versa.

In this section, you'll find plenty of clues on how to improve your approach to what you write as well as your writing techniques. Make a habit of using words that "hook" and understand the importance of using a call to action in every piece. Then, in the final stages, use the tips included here to better proofread what you've written.

In this section, you'll learn about:

- **Think in the prospect's perspective**
- **Capturing customers with persuasive words**
- **Marketing writing that gets read**
- **How to improve your proofreading skills**

Think in the Prospect's Perspective

Marketing expert Julie Wassom of The Julian Group, Inc. emphasizes the importance of thinking in the prospect's perspective. She recommends you consider a key question to use as a guide before creating your marketing pieces.

"How does this piece serve *me*?"

That's the key question in the minds of your prospects and customers when they read your brochure, glance through your newsletter, or visit your website.

When you "think in the prospect's perspective," consider the relevance of the marketing messages you communicate. Your prospects are already asking, "What does this mean to me?" and "How will this help me?"

Each time they see or hear a marketing message from you, they think about the benefits they'll receive from your product or services. The benefits they perceive they'll gain affect their buying decisions.

Here are three ways to float to the top when you're swimming in a sea of too many marketing messages competing with yours.

1. **Think value.** When you put together an informational piece on your website or in print, don't sign off on it until you can state at least three ways your prospects will perceive it as being valuable to them. Advertising is necessary, but often is perceived by prospects as merely *promoting you* rather than *assisting them*. Copy that includes "benefits" versus "features" can help change that perception.

2. **Provide relevant free information to position yourself as a helpful expert and to encourage a dialogue with your prospects.** Does your website have a page from which visitors can download tips, articles of interest, or a list of helpful resources? Does the information change periodically so visitors retain interest in returning to your site? If not, start making some changes.

3. **Look for the little things that other methods miss.**
Personal contact, for instance. Does your follow-up program include a periodic call to prospects so you can answer questions, invite them to preview your services, or just be there as a helpful resource? It may sound simple or old-fashioned, but the call builds a relationship that sells like nothing else can.

Remember, clients and customers are thinking, "How does this serve me?" Serve them well and your efforts will be well rewarded in sales and referrals.

© 2005 by Julie Wassom, 303-693-2306, www.juliewassom.com. All rights reserved, used by permission.

Sources of relevant free information on a website

Capturing Customers with Persuasive Words

To create marketing pieces that catch your prospective customers' attention, use sharp direct "hooks" that persuade them to take action.

Does Your Piece Tell or Sell?

In addition to appealing graphics, the actual words used in your piece serve as critical hooks because they persuade the prospect to further investigate your product or service.

When writing the copy, it's a common mistake to dwell on the features of a product or service rather than how those features make a difference to potential buyers. If you're selling the concept of breeding alpacas as a business, for example, writing about the characteristics of the animals themselves won't motivate prospects to buy them. Instead, you stress what having alpacas will do for *your customers*—e.g., create a better lifestyle, give them tax advantages and retirement income, and so on. Spelling out desirable changes they'll experience from breeding alpacas has a good chance of motivating them to take the next step toward purchasing from you.

12 Words That Persuade

Using persuasive words in your marketing pieces goes a long way toward hooking your prospects. A Yale University study on auditory persuasiveness deemed the following 12 words the most persuasive ones in the English language:

discovery	easy
guarantee	love
health	money
new	proven
results	safety
save	you

Consciously use these key persuasive words to add impact to your marketing piece.

Always Include a Call to Action

Following the benefits stated in your piece, write a phrase—a call to action—that tells your prospects exactly what to do next. Make sure the wording in your call to action commands action. Merely being informative isn't enough; your call to action statement must be directive.

Eye-Popping Tip. *Example of directive wording: "Call today to schedule a time to meet." Example of informative wording: "We welcome you to call us."*

When you use a call to action, you'll find that a high percentage of prospects do exactly what you ask them to. Use these phrases as models to write your own call to action.

- Visit our website today for _____.
- Call _____ for an appointment NOW.
- Contact us at _____.
- Watch for updates at _____.

Choose both words and graphics that make your call to action stand out in every marketing piece you create.

Creating a Sense of Urgency

What can your copy say that would encourage your prospects to take action NOW?

Again, you can create urgency with the words you use, highlighted by how you make them stand out on the page. Appeal to a basic human fear of loss by using phrases that make them believe they might lose out. Here are a few phrases that hook:

- Offer expires on_____.
- Your last chance is coming!
- Call by _____ before it's too late!

3 Critical Elements

1. **Be bold.** Whether it's your design, the colors or photos you choose, or your copy itself, push the envelope in these areas. When you do, it helps make your ad jump off the page.

2. **Less is best.** Use lots of white space, bullets, a strong headline, and a directive call to action statement that stand out in your piece. If it looks crowded, it won't get read.

3. **Accentuate your website address.** These days, most prospects who are intrigued by your piece follow up by checking your website. Make sure the web address can't be missed by using large bold type or a complementary color.

You have a lot of hooks at your fingertips to make your ad both eye-catching and exceptional. Be sure to use them every time!

© 2005 by Julie Wassom, 303-693-2306, www.juliewassom.com. All rights reserved, used by permission.

Marketing Writing That Gets Read

If you pay attention to these tips on good writing from Barbara McNichol, you'll start to think like an editor and your marketing pieces will come across in a professional way.

Ever been lured into reading a brochure with graphics that promise blue skies, sunshine, and unlimited happiness? When you eyeball this piece, you're compelled to find out more but become disappointed when you actually read it. You've been drawn into a lackluster description of a product you don't understand and have to wade through long-winded sentences to get the point!

On the other hand, you may have tossed aside a boring-looking brochure until a friend persuaded you to dive into the information. This piece offers a product you want in a way that addresses your pain now. You could have missed it!

Eye-Popping Tip. *Just as love and marriage go together, so do good design and good writing. Good design draws attention to the message of a piece, while effective writing/editing communicates it in words. Together, they make the difference between a piece getting actively read or passively tossed.*

What Makes a Difference?

What concepts make the most difference in writing your marketing pieces?

- Know who you are writing for; keep their preferences in mind as you write each word.

- Put the message in terms of "you" rather than "I" or "we." People don't care about what "we" offer; they care about how "you" can make their lives better.

- Make it clear what your readers should do, think, or believe as a result of reading the information presented.

With these concepts in mind, sit down and write the most clear, persuasive piece of text that you can. Seem intimidating? It's not when you adopt these techniques for improving your writing.

1. Make verbs dance.
Which of these two sentences has more liveliness?
Passive — "The juicy watermelon was eaten by the boy."
Active — "The boy chomped into the watermelon's belly, enjoying each juicy bite."

2. Get agreements.
When you put a singular subject with the plural form of the verb, you weaken your writing, confuse your reader, and make grammarians groan. Example sentence: "A group of writers were in town." Note that the subject of the sentence, "group," is singular while the verb "were" belongs with a plural subject. Instead, write this: "A group of writers was in town" or "Several writers were in town." Better yet, liven up the sentence with an active verb: "A group of writers landed in town" or another more imaginative verb.

However, beware of verb agreements using the subject "none" as in: "None of the writers were in town." In this case, "were" is correct because "none" means "not any of the writers." Therefore, none is a plural subject requiring the plural form of the verb.

3. Watch for mixed modifiers.
"When thinking about a good place to eat, many choices are available." Are the "many choices" doing the thinking? I don't think so! Mixed modifiers and dangling participles get in the way of crisp, intentional communication. Write this instead: "When thinking about a good place to eat, the organizer had many choices." It's now clear who is doing the thinking—the organizer!

4. Stay on a parallel path.
Don't let a mixed bag of structures wiggle its way into your writing. Here's what I mean by mixed structure: "His attitude makes a difference in changing, succeeding, and when he wants to move on." Instead, the sentence should be: "His attitude makes a difference in changing, succeeding, and moving on."

5. Choose the perfect word when it matters most.

Do you write "further" when you mean "farther" or "accept" instead of "except?" Selecting the right word avoids confusion for the reader and embarrassment for you. Keep a reference guide handy to clarify trick combos such as *than* vs. *then* and *stationery* vs. *stationary*.

© 2005 by Barbara McNichol, www.BarbaraMcNichol.com, 877-696-4899, All rights reserved. Used by permission.

How to Improve Your Proofreading Skills

What Gets In the Way?
The ego is the biggest hindrance to proofreading your own work well. Because it assumes accuracy, it can influence the mind to overlook typos.

Here's evidence from researchers at Texas A&M University:

> **Spelling and the Brain:**
>
> Aoccdrnig to rscheearch at Txes M&A Uinervtisy, it doesn't Mttaer in what order the ltteers in a word are, the only iprmoetnt thing is taht the first and lsat ltteer be in the rghit pclae. The rset can be a total mses and you can still raed it wouthit a porbelm. This is bcuseae the huamn mind deos not raed ervey lteter by istlef, but the word as a wlohe.

The first impression a business often makes with prospective clients or customers comes from the written word. Your company can lose credibility by having just one typo in the volumes of words it sends out.

Therefore, to minimize mistakes, be sure to proofread everything that gets written in your office—and this includes email. Use a guide to help you methodically check for errors. Avoid proofing your own copy in the final stages because it's easy to become too familiar with it. If it isn't feasible to delegate proofreading, leave the copy alone for a while—a day preferably—before searching for errors. Read it backwards, too. It's a good way to trick your mind into seeing common mistakes.

Read Copy Four Times

I recommend rereading your copy four times:

- The first time, check for deviations in text, e.g., words typed twice in a row (the the), typographical errors, and incorrect word breaks. For example, consider an erroneous word break that's made with the word "therapist." If this word is hyphenated in the wrong place, it becomes the "the-rapist." That doesn't leave a good impression!

- The second time, read for fact or format inconsistency, poor word usage, weak sentence structure, subject/verb disagreements, repetition of thoughts or phrases, and incorrect math.

- On the third read, check for language mechanics such as capitalization, punctuation, spelling, and grammar.

- The fourth read includes checking overall format—type size, margins, alignment, spacing, positioning (headlines, subheads, copy, footnotes, indentations), pagination, and general appearance.

Eye-Popping Tip. *When you set aside time to proofread your piece, you'll avoid costly mistakes and leave your prospects with a positive first impression.*

Writing Persuasive Content And Making It Flow

Some Common Proofreading Marks

Example	Meaning
good typesetting	Upper case
GOOD Typesettting lc.	Lower case
Good typesetting ital.	Italics
Good typesetting bf	Boldface
Goood typesetting	Delete
Typesetting Good	Transpose
Good typesetting ⊙	Insert period
Good typesetting ⁁ ,/	Insert comma
⁁Good typesetting" ''/	Insert open quote
"Good typesetting⁁ ''/	Insert close quote
Good typesetting⁁ ?	Insert question mark
Good typesetting⁁ !	Insert exclamation point
Good⁁typesetting =	Insert hyphen
Good typesetting⁁ ;/	Insert Semicolon
¶Good typesetting	New paragraph
Good⁁typesetting #	Insert space
Good typesetting⁁ …	Insert ellipsis
Good *typesetting* wf	Wrong font
Good (typesetting) Rom	Roman
Good type setting	Close up
]Good typesetting[	Center
Good (tipesetting) sp	Spelling
▢Good typesetting	Indent
]Good typesetting	Move to the right
[Good typesetting	Move to the left
Good typesetting stet.	Let it stand (ignore changes)

37

The Best Typography For Design And Readability

Good design incorporates a skilled use of typography, which refers to the look and arrangement of type as it's used in a layout. Not only does good typography make the design attractive, it's simply easier to read.

In this section, you'll learn more about:

- **Start with the ABCs**
- **Legibility and readability of fonts**
- **Choosing fonts**
- **How to match your font to your message**
- **Setting the tone of your text with kerning, tracking, and leading**
- **9 typesetting tricks that design pros use**
- **Shopping for types of fonts**

Start with the ABCs

Once you improve your understanding of typography, you'll be able to make better choices of the font (a complete set of characters and symbols that comprise one typeface) you want to use in your eye-catching pieces.

Parts of a Letter
A discussion of typography starts with the key basic component—the letter—and extends to symbols, numbers, and other elements that make up a font. Font designs vary because the proportions of the letters used vary from font to font. Proportions are determined by cap height, x-height, ascenders, and descenders of the letters, as indicated below. Do you notice that some fonts appear small for their type size? This is usually because they have small x-heights.

The illustrations below explain the parts of the letter, and x-height ratio.

Cap Height — Right Type — Ascender / X-Height / Descender
Baseline →

Do you see how looks can be deceiving? Both examples below are set in 72-point type. Bodoni has a smaller x-height ratio than Cheltenham, therefore it looks smaller.

Bodoni font 72 point — Specify — Small X-Height

Cheltenham font 72 point — Specify — Large X-Height

Legibility and Readability of Fonts

Legibility refers to the clarity of the type character—how easily it is identified. Readability refers to how some fonts are more suited for long sections of body copy. Body copy needs to be legible and readable while display type (headlines) just needs to be legible.

The fonts you choose and how you use them affect the legibility of your design. Stylized, decorative, condensed, and expanded fonts are much more difficult to read than standard fonts. The simple, clean design of Garamond font makes it easier to read than the three other examples below.

Garamond
MESQUITE   *Brush Script*   Viva

Readability of All-Capital Letters

Generally speaking, using all capital letters (ALL CAPS) affects readability in a negative way. That's why it's best to use upper and lower case for blocks of text.

Notice how difficult it is to read the paragraph below set in all caps.

GENERALLY SPEAKING, USING ALL CAPITAL LETTERS (ALL CAPS) AFFECTS READABILITY IN A NEGATIVE WAY. THAT'S WHY IT'S BEST TO USE UPPER AND LOWER CASE FOR BLOCKS OF TEXT.

Reserve the all-capital setting for special cases when just a few words are emphasized.

Eye-Popping Tip: *In a Word document, you can highlight a section of copy and press Shift-F3 to quickly change the highlighted text from lower case to upper case and back.*

Choosing Fonts

A quick look on your software reveals myriad choices of fonts and you can always find more! But like shopping in a candy store, you have to make judicious selections. Before you do, take a moment to understand the characteristics of fonts, including sizes, types, and much more.

Times **Arial**

Serif

Serif vs. Sans Serif Fonts

Serifs are the tiny marks or horizontal strokes attached to some of the fonts; sans serif refers to fonts that don't have horizontal strokes or serifs. "Sans" is from the French word "without." Sans serif means "no serifs."

A serif font such as Times Roman is better suited for body copy because the letterforms are easily distinguished and the horizontal strokes (serifs) on the ends of the letterforms help the reader's eye flow from letter to letter. Arial is a good example of a sans serif font, and is well suited for headlines and subheads. (See examples on the left.)

Sizes of Fonts

Type size is based on a measurement system called points and picas. A point is 1/72 of an inch. A pica is 12 points or 1/6 of an inch. Points are used to specify type size while picas, being a larger measurement, are used for line length and column depth.

Be sure to select a font size that is appropriate to your readers; older readers and children require a larger font size for text—preferably type size 12, 13, or larger.

Type Family

To give your layout a unified look, I recommend that you limit the number of fonts you use. It is best to use one font (preferably a **bold** one) for your headlines and another font family for the body copy. (A family is all the related styles that come with the font, and usually include **bold,** *italic,* and ***bold italic.***) You can use italics or bold variations within the family for pull quotes or call-outs, captions, and sidebars. (See Jazz Up Your Layouts With Pull Quotes.)

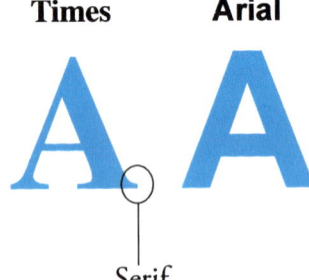

How to Match Your Font to Your Message

Try These for Headlines

Helvetica Bold

Gill Sans Bold

Eras Bold

Univers Black

Franklin Gothic Demi

Try These for Body Copy

Garamond

Caslon

Goudy

Stone Print

New Century Schoolbook

Janson Text 55 Roman

It is important to select appropriate fonts to communicate your message to your readers, particularly when dealing with titles and headlines. Why? Because specific fonts can evoke a certain attitude and feeling that reinforces your intended message.

Fonts for Headlines

Choose a bold font with the right personality for your piece. Some common bold fonts are Helvetica Bold, Gill Sans Bold, Eras Bold, Univers Black, and Franklin Gothic Demi. Here are some more sample fonts and their personalities:

Jazzy	Country	Elegant
MILITARY	Playful	Assertive
Childlike	Sci-Fi	CLASSIC

Fonts for Body Copy

The font you use for your body copy can have some personality, but make sure it is readable. Some standard-proportion serif fonts with medium x-heights that are good choices for body copy are Garamond, Caslon, Goudy, Stone Print, New Century Schoolbook, and Janson Text 55 Roman. (See examples on the left.)

Eye-Popping Tip: *For headlines, you'll find that using a contrasting font for your copy adds visual interest and balance. A good combination of fonts would be Garamond Regular for text and Myriad Bold for heads as was used in this guide.*

This is a sample of 12 point Myriad Bold used for the subheads in this book. The heads (chapter titles) are 24 point.

This is a sample of 12 point Adobe Garamond Regular used for the body copy in this book.

Setting the Tone of Your Text with Kerning, Tracking, and Leading

The relationship of the text to its surrounding space is important. For example, your layout will look choppy and be difficult to read if you use too much white space between words and lines of type. Alternatively, text that is set too tight is also difficult to read. This factor is called setting the "tone" of your text. Having the right tone ensures readability.

Quite often when you look closely at a block of text, you'll notice that the way letters are spaced automatically doesn't take into account the individual letter shapes or relationships of characters. As a result, the text has uneven white spaces and looks unbalanced. Your goal is to create an even rhythm of letters, words, and white space for best readability.

How do you control the tone? With kerning, tracking, leading, and line length commands. Kerning is the process of adding or subtracting space between specific pairs of characters, usually in headlines. Tracking is the process of loosening or tightening a block of text.

Kerning—the spatial relationship between letters

The examples below show how designers can manually change the relationship between pairs of letters using kerning. Notice the difference in the space between the letters "V" and "A" and also "T" and "A." (Kerning is usually available in design and drawing programs, and may not be available in your word processing program.)

Before manual kerning:

ADVANTAGE

After manual kerning:

ADVANTAGE

Tracking

> **An example of tight tracking**
>
> Tatum quatisi. Duismodiat, veniam vendip et lore eum am, venissis aliquat, sit ad et non ex et, si. Aciliquatis do consequisis ea faccum nos er sum zzril il dolortis exercilisl et iurerciduis nonsequat.

> **An example of loose (open) tracking**
>
> Tatum quatisi. Duismodiat, veniam vendip et lore eum am, venissis aliquat, sit ad et non ex et, si. Aciliquatis do consequisis ea faccum nos er sum zzril il dolortis exercilisl et iurer.

Leading—the space between lines

Also affecting the design and readability of your text is the leading (or linespacing), which is a measure of the space between lines of copy.

The term "leading" comes from the metal type era when printers inserted a lead bar between the lead slugs of type to increase the spacing between lines.

Leading is measured in point increments and specified in conjunction with the point size of the font. For example, 10/12 (read 10 on 12) is 10-point type with 12 point leading. In most cases, the leading of body copy should be about 120% of the point size of the text. (For example 10/12 or 12/14.4.)

Make sure you set your leading in proportion to the line length of your text. In general, short lines of type require little or no extra leading but you should increase the leading as you increase the length of the line.

Eye-Popping Tip: *The examples shown on this page and the following page use "Greeking Copy" or "Placeholder Text" as a way to represent paragraphs of text without having the actual copy. Some page layout programs have this feature listed in the "Type" menu.*

An example of 10 point text on 10 point leading in a narrow column

Lorem ipsum dolor sit amet, consectetuer adipiscing elit, sed diam nonummy nibh euismod tincidunt ut laoreet dolore magna aliquam erat volutpat. Ut wisi enim ad minim veniam, quis nostrud exerci tation ullamcorper suscipit lobortis nisl ut aliquip ex ea commodo consequat. Duis autem vel eum iriure dolor in hendrerit in vulputate velit esse molestie consequat, vel illum dolore eu feugait nulla facilisis at vero eros et accumsan et iusto odio dignissim qui blandit praesent luptatum zzril delenit augue duis dolore te feugait nulla

An Example of 12 Point Text on 14.4 Point Leading in a Medium Width Column

Lorem ipsum dolor sit amet, consectetuer adipiscing elit, sed diam nonummy nibh euismod tincidunt ut laoreet dolore magna aliquam erat volutpat. Ut wisi enim ad minim veniam, quis nostrud exerci tation ullamcorper suscipit lobortis nisl ut aliquip ex ea commodo consequat. Duis autem vel eum iriure dolor in hendrerit in vulputate velit esse molestie consequat, vel illum dolore eu feugiat nulla facilisis at vero eros et accumsan et iusto odio dignissim qui blandit praesent luptatum zzril delenit augue duis dolore te feugait nulla facilisi. Lorem ipsum dolor sit amet, consectetuer adipiscing elit, sed diam nonummy nibh euismod tincidunt ut laoreet dolore magna aliquam erat volutpat. Adipiscing elit, sed diam nonummy nibh euismod tincidunt ut laoreet dolore magna aliquam erat volutpat. Duis autem vel eum iriure dolor in hendrerit in vulputate velit esse molestie.

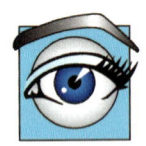

Eye-Popping Tip: *For headlines, I recommend using leading that is equal to or less than the point size of the type being used in the text. This creates a tighter, more cohesive look that makes the headline more readable.*

This is an example of Helvetica Bold headline set 24/24

Paragraph Alignment

Some blocks of copy (such as this paragraph) are full justified, which means the type is spaced in a way that both the left and right margins are straight and all lines are the same length.

Using justified type makes a page look full and creates a tighter, more formal appearance than type that is not full justified. Most books are set with full justified copy, because the reader's eye can move more quickly across copy that has a consistent column width.

> **Example of full justified copy**
> Lorem ipsum dolor sit amet, consectetuer adipiscing elit, sed diam nonummy nibh euismod tincidunt ut laoreet dolore magna aliquam erat volutpat. Ut wisi enim ad minim veniam, quis nostrud exerci tation ullamcorper.

Copy that is set with a "flush" margin on one side and a "ragged" margin on the other side (for example, flush left/ragged right) has a friendlier, less formal look than full justified type. However, it may be more difficult to read because the eye is tripped up by the irregular right margin. The reverse of flush left/ragged right is flush right/ragged left. This combination is even more difficult to read and is rarely used in large blocks of text.

> **Example of flush left/ragged right copy**
> Lorem ipsum dolor sit amet, consectetuer adipiscing elit, sed diam nonummy nibh euismod tincidunt ut laoreet dolore magna aliquam erat volutpat. Ut wisi enim ad minim veniam, quis nostrud exerci tation ullamcorper.

Centered copy is generally reserved for formal announcements, headings, subheads, or pull quotes within the text. It also is difficult to read because of the ever-changing line lengths. I recommend using it sparingly; that's when it works most effectively.

> **Example of centered copy**
> Lorem ipsum dolor sit amet, consectetuer adipiscing elit, sed diam nonummy nibh euismod tincidunt ut laoreet dolore magna aliquam erat volutpat. Ut wisi enim ad minim veniam, quis nostrud exerci tation ullamcorper.

Eye-Popping Tip: *Smaller type works best at shorter line lengths, while a larger type size is readable in a wide column length. For most blocks of text, the line length should be between 40 and 65 characters.*

9 Typesetting Tricks That Design Pros Use

The better your typeset pages look, the easier it is for readers to grasp the information on those pages. Paying special attention to small details makes the difference between your pages looking amateur or professional.

Here are 9 time-honored tricks that design pros use.

Paragraph Indents
Set the distance for indenting your paragraphs equal to the point size of your text. For example, if you use a 14-point text, you'd set up a 14-point indent (about 3/16").

Single Space after Punctuation
In the old days of using typewriters, it was necessary to put two spaces at the end of a sentence or after a colon because the width of all the characters was fixed, not variable. Nowadays, because computer fonts have built-in proportional spacing, you only need one space. If you type in two spaces, it leaves too large of a gap in the line of type. Leave your "two spaces" habit behind!

Word Emphasis
It may have been customary to underline words for emphasis in the past, but designers today simply don't use it. Visually, it looks much better to *italicize* or **bold** the words you want to emphasize.

Example of an Em Dash:

She swam one mile—he biked twelve miles.

Examples of an En Dash:

January 15–August 20
8:00–10:00

Hyphens and Dashes
In the past, typewriters required using two hyphens to make a dash. In today's typesetting, it's more professional to replace two hyphens with a long "em" dash (which is the square of the type body size—for example 14 point size text would have a 14 point with em dash.) A smaller dash but still longer than a hyphen is called an "en" dash (1/2 the length of em dash). You'd use an "em" dash to separate out a phrase in a sentence and an "en" dash for dates and times (see examples on the left).

The Best Typography For Design And Readability

We are about there...

Two separate pairs of letters

Two common ligatures

Ellipsis
An ellipsis refers to the three periods commonly used in a text to indicate a pause or missing words. Designers find that the single keystroke command for an ellipsis spaces the dots too close together. Instead, they manually type "space-dot-space-dot-space-dot-space" for a more professional look.

Ligatures
A "ligature" is two letters combined as one special character. Most fonts have these two common ligature combinations: fl and fi. If you typed these letters separately, the two letters almost touch one another. The ligature makes the two letters fit together better, and is considered very fine typography. Ligatures look particularly attractive when set as italic in a serif font (see examples on the left). Most new fonts, when used with professional page layout or drawing programs, will automatically create some ligatures. Other fonts require a special combination of keyboard strokes. A complete set of glyphs and more exotic ligatures is accessable using the "Glyphs" command in the "Type" pulldown menu.

Widows and Orphans
When one word or part of one word remains on a line by itself at the end of a paragraph, designers call it a "widow." Although having widows in a text is technically acceptable, designers consider them to be undesirable. You can eliminate them by adjusting the tracking in the paragraph. However, it's both undesirable and unacceptable to have an "orphan," which is the last word of the previous paragraph all by itself at the top the next column. You can also eliminate orphans by adjusting the tracking or by removing a word or two.

Susan said, "Brenda's car is red."

Tom is 5' 10" tall.

Quotation Marks, Inches and Feet, and Apostrophes
A sure way to tell if type was set by a pro is to look at the quotation marks in the text. Pros make sure the opening and closing quotation marks are "curly" shapes while the marks used to abbreviate feet and inches are "straight." Always use the single "curly" mark and not the "straight" mark for apostrophes. Your page layout program should give you both options, so use them correctly (see examples on the left).

Hanging Indents

Numbered and bulleted lists are much easier to read when you set them with a hanging indent and put an extra space between the items, as the example shows. When type is set this way, individual items are separated from one another and therefore easier to read. The term "hanging indent" means aligning the second line of type with the first line of type, not with the bullet or number. You can set your program to do this automatically.

An Example of a Hanging Indent

Book cover design requires instant eye appeal. Good designers achieve this by:

- Using bold graphics and colors

- Exploring imagery to depict the book's personality

- Designing simply and elegantly . . . without clutter

- Creating a perfect "fit" for the market niche

Shopping for Types of Fonts

Open Type

The best type of font to buy is an OpenType font. This is the newest type of font, designed to work on both a Macintosh and a PC. The OpenType fonts contain many ligatures, fractions, and decorative dingbats in addition to the standard alphabet and numbers.

I recommend always buying a font in a family (usually regular, *italic,* **bold,** and ***bold italic,*** and sometimes more) unless it is a special decorative type of font. You'll want to use several members of the family in your layouts. They especially come in handy when you want to emphasize certain words or phrases in a sentence.

Check that your computer operating system and program version are compatible with the OpenType fonts; some older computers and operating systems are not. The next best font to buy is a PostScript font or Type 1 font, especially if you are sending your PDF or page layout files to the printer to be offset printed.

True Type

Another common type of font is called TrueType font. However, TrueType fonts have been known to cause problems in typesetting equipment. (Typesetting equipment is the prepress equipment used to convert your file to the printing plate or film negative.)

Generally, the typesetting equipment is set up to work with PostScript fonts. TrueType is not PostScript font, but TrueType fonts are popular and widely used because they're included with purchases of Microsoft Office and the Macintosh operating system. They are fine to use in office-related tasks.

Adobe products (PageMaker, InDesign, Photoshop, Illustrator) have always included free fonts that are PostScript, Type 1, or OpenType. Adobe fonts may be more expensive than others, but you'll find they are of higher quality. Adobe pays the license fees to the original artist or foundry, and painstakingly renders them as accurate to the original as possible. And Adobe builds complex kerning tables and glyphs that many other companies don't.

You can buy PostScript, Type 1, or OpenType fonts from www.adobe.com or other places online. In fact, you can pay for and download a variety of fonts directly from websites that sell them.

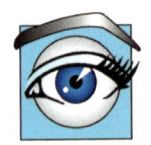

Eye-Popping Tip: *If you have seen a font that you particularly like, but don't know what it's called, you can get help at www.myfonts.com. Email a sample of the font and, for no charge, you'll get a response telling you its name.*

Laying Out Your Pages With Style

Look in a newsletter or magazine that's professionally designed, then contrast it with an amateur desktop publisher's work. Doing this will help you identify many of the techniques that professional designers use.

In this section, you'll learn more about:

- **6 elements that make your design effective**
- **The magic of working with grids**
- **Working with images to enhance your layout**
- **Jazz up your layouts with pull quotes**
- **A checklist of features that add eye appeal**

6 Elements that Make Your Design Effective

In today's market, your customers and clients are influenced more than ever by the visual presentation of your marketing materials. If your marketing piece is well designed, it is likely to be read, remembered, and respected.

As you create your own materials, be sure to apply these basic design concepts and ideas to do the job effectively:

1. Serif and Sans Serif Fonts
In general, when you have a large amount of text, it is best to use a serif font because it is easier to read than a sans serif font. Use sans serif fonts (usually in bold) for subheads and headlines. Some examples of serif fonts are: Times, New Century Schoolbook, Garamond and Goudy. Some examples of Sans Serif fonts are: Arial, Helvetica, Univers and Trade Gothic. (See Choosing Fonts.)

2. Clip Art and Stock Photos
Chances are you're not an illustrator or photographer, but that shouldn't stop you from using professional illustrations in your marketing piece. You can use clip art—sometimes at a very low price—to enhance your layout. (Check out the Internet for sites that feature clip art or stock photo libraries that provide a wide variety of quality and prices to choose from.) Match clip art you select with the "style" of graphics so you create a consistent look and feel on the page. Two sources for photos are www.photos.com and www.istockphoto.com.

3. Contrast
Using contrast means having clearly apparent differences among the design elements that come together on a page, business card, or computer screen. These include contrasting colors, shapes, fonts, and sizes of text and graphics. A high degree of contrast helps create dramatic interest and draws the viewer's eye to specific areas of your page. White space also provides contrast, aids legibility, and gives the reader's eye a resting point. Controlling the amount of white space you use affects the overall page design.

Laying Out Your Pages With Style

This flyer uses several of these design elements: Contrast in size (the letters M,O,R,E, and the two suns). Repetition is shown in the treatment of the typography in each paragraph. The large sun in the lower right balances the weight of the large letters on the left side and the top photo.

4. Repetition

Good design calls for repeating certain elements throughout your piece to make the whole piece come together visually. For example, use the same color, shape, and size for all your bullets. Also make all your headers the same size, color, and font. Go for more and repeat specific graphic elements (e.g., boxes, banners, rule lines, etc.) throughout the piece. A word of caution: When you review your work, make sure you've used all of these design elements consistently.

5. Alignment

To create a sense of balance and alignment in your piece, use a tool called a grid. (See The Magic of Working with Grids.) Follow the grid lines to position your text, graphics, and photos—in effect, creating invisible straight lines that align these elements and give the piece a visual sense of order. If you "almost" align items, then the piece looks sloppy and chaotic, not professional.

6. Proximity

Proximity refers to the exact spatial relationships between elements. For example, you create visual relationships between photos and their captions by keeping the captions close to the photos. For subheads, a professional positions them closer to the text below than the text above. Apply this principle of exact spatial relationship to all other graphic and text elements where appropriate. When you review your work, make sure you've applied this spacing consistently throughout.

Use these six elements and you'll draw positive attention to your marketing piece every time!

Maximize. . .
Your memory with **Total Recall** ©
Did you know you have a photographic memory?

Learn: How to remember people's names, presentation materials and important statistics.

Organize. . .
Your life with **Priority Shuffle** ©
Did you know you can organize your life in 15 minutes a day?

Learn: Task management strategies that guarantee success!

Realize. . .
Your full potential with
Coaching for Today's Leader's ©
Did you know the greatest coach lies within you?

Learn: How to develop tomorrow's leaders, TODAY!

Energize. . .
Your teams with **Jumpstart Your TQ** ©
You have an IQ and an EQ . . .
Did you know you have a TQ as well?

Learn: How to create powerful, effective teams.

Marguerite Ham

Become MORE
with Marguerite Ham

The Magic of Working with Grids

Are your page layouts messy and unorganized? Don't know where to start when designing your page layout?

Here's a secret tool that designers have used for years—the "grid." A grid provides logical positions for placing text and graphics. Create a simple grid such as one of the two samples shown here. If your software has the option, use non-printing guidelines to indicate your grid units.

Place Your Text and Graphics

Generally, keep the content inside the grid units and out of the margins, gutter, and alleys. The longest line of text should be no longer than the grid width. Text and graphics may horizontally or vertically span one, two, or more grids. For an interesting effect, it's okay if an *occasional irregular* object or shape aggressively "hangs out" over the edge of the grid unit.

Two Sample Grids
Each of these small-scale "thumbnails" represent a 2-page spread. The thin lines represent the grid lines, the edge of the page, and the centerfold.

Sample 2-page, 2-column grid

Sample 2-page, 6-unit grid

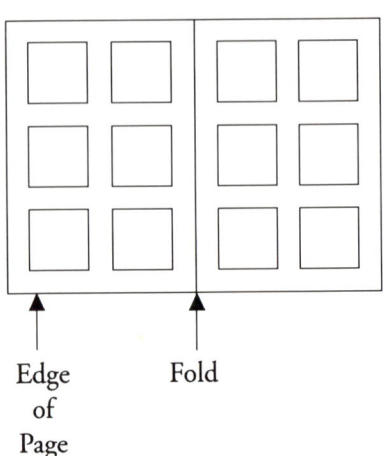

Gutter
Alley   Alley
Margin   Margin
Edge of Page   Fold

Laying Out Your Pages With Style

Four Different Looks

Using the identical 6-unit grid, you can create many interesting variations. Photos or graphics expand to fill 2- and 3-unit horizontal grids or a large photo can fill four complete units. Notice how photos or graphics can extend across alleys. You can "bleed" or run the photos off the edge of the page or "butt" them against the fold line in the gutter. All grid units do not have to be filled. This creates "white space" that adds interest to the layout and draws the eye to important areas. Notice how the grid and its visual order are still apparent.

2-Page Spread #1

Page 1   Page 2

2-Page Spread #2

Page 1   Page 2

2-Page Spread #3

Page 1   Page 2

2-Page Spread #4

Page 1   Page 2

The "thumbnails" above show four different spreads. **Please note:** *The solid black areas represent photos, illustrations, or color boxes filled with text or bulleted items. The thick horizontal gray lines represent text.*

Working with Images to Enhance Your Layout

The old adage asserts, "One picture is worth a thousand words." Because of a photo's ability to make an impact, choose yours wisely. In fact, photos and illustrations work best when used with the intention of adding to the reader's understanding.

To add to their innate impact, follow these rules of thumb for cropping and placing your photos and illustrations in your marketing piece.

- Place your strongest image in the top half of the page where it will get the best visibility. This is especially important in full-page magazine ads.

- One large picture makes a stronger impression than several smaller ones.

- If you do use several small pictures, group them together so that they collectively form a single, compact element.

- An asymmetrical arrangement is livelier and looks better than balancing pictures in matching positions on opposite corners of a page.

- Experiment with juxtaposing a small picture with a much larger one for contrast.

- Try to place the image as close as possible to the text that relates to it (i.e., on the same page or column).

- Use your column grid or ruler guides to line up the images, and "break out" of the grid occasionally for added interest.

- When placing several headshots in one document, try to scale all photos so that all the heads are about the same size.

- Simplify a cluttered background by airbrushing out unwanted or distracting elements.

- Zoom in on your subject to focus on the important visual elements. This is called "cropping." (See example at left.)

- Experiment with silhouettes or "break outs" by eliminating the entire background of your photo.

Original Photo

Cropped Photo
Notice that when the unnecessary items are cropped out of the photo, the focus turns to the couple and their car.

Laying Out Your Pages With Style

Handling Your Photos and Illustrations

- Don't write on the front or back of the photo or illustration. It may rub off on the front of another one stacked on it.

- Don't use paper clips on photos; they can scratch the emulsion. Never staple a photo or illustration.

- Write on a Post-It®, then place the Post-It® on the photo to avoid making an impression on the photo's emulsion.

- Never trim the actual photograph or illustration. Scan the entire image and use computer software to crop and trim the image.

For additional information on organizing and scanning your photos, determining the proper file formats and resolution, see Working With Digital Imagery in this guide.

Original Photo   *"Silhouette" Photo*

Jazz Up Your Layouts with Pull Quotes

Break up monotonous lines of text with attractive "pull quotes" or "call-outs." To do so, just copy a provocative or challenging statement from your text and paste it into a different position with larger, contrasting type. Add decorative quotation marks (see examples), border it with lines, or place it inside a box.

This is a sample pull quote using bold opening and closing quotation marks.

Pull quotes add graphic interest to a layout and make important information visible at a glance. The small-scale thumbnails illustrated on the following page show three different positions for pull quotes on a page layout. The rectangle outline represents the edge of the page and the gray horizontal lines represent text.

The examples shown here and on the following page are basic pull quote designs. All can be embellished and modified. For example, try using different icons for the large quotation marks. Simple, bold characters from the "Dingbats" font (usually included on most computers) are fun.

These are a few Dingbats:

Also experiment with line thickness, types of lines, multiple lines, reversed-out lettering (dark colored box with white lettering), and color tints.

This is a sample pull quote using a drop shadow box.

Laying Out Your Pages With Style

This is a sample pull quote with rule lines.

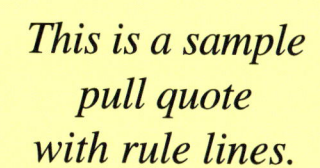

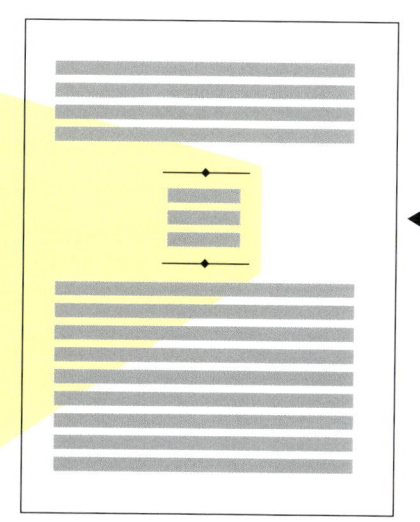

◀ *Indent on both sides with lots of space above and below the quote. Note how this pull quote has decorative rule lines above and below it.*

◀ *You can "cut" the quote into the text column, but let it "hang out" on a wide white margin. Use a different font than the body text.*

◀ *Place the quote between two columns of text and frame it with a box. You can fill the box with a light color or tint.*

A Checklist of Features that Add Eye Appeal

Remember, you've set out to add eye appeal that makes your company stand out in the eyes of your target audience. Here's a good opportunity to summarize key points to keep in mind as you proceed with your design.

1. Let One Thing Dominate
When you look at a well-designed ad or direct mail piece, usually one dominant feature will catch your eye. It could be the headline or the picture, but usually not both. Something has to dominate. If you try to emphasize *everything,* you'll end up emphasizing *nothing.*

2. Minimize Font Variety
Your computer may come with 327 fonts, but that doesn't mean you have to use every single one of them. The best designers stick to one, or maybe two fonts per piece. A good rule of thumb is to use large, bold type for headlines. Use a smaller easy-to-read font for text. (See Typography section for more details.)

3. Become a Fan of White Space
Don't feel compelled to fill every inch of space with copy or pictures. A page full of dense type and pictures can look unattractive and turn readers away. An open and airy design is more inviting and easier to read.

4. Design Easy-to-Read Layouts
Equally important as the overall design of the page is the design of the specific text blocks. If the type is too small or condensed, if the columns are too wide, if the paragraphs are too long, it becomes too much work for the reader. This applies to letters and emails too. Break up copy with indents, bullet points, or bold subheads.

5. Use Relevant Illustrations
An illustration or picture can help draw attention to or dramatize your message. Illustrations can be descriptive, dramatic, or comical, but should be relevant to the message in the piece.

This chapter is used with permission from The Print Council: The Printing Industries of America, Inc.

Laying Out Your Pages With Style

6. Include Logo, Contact Information, and Call to Action

Okay. You captured the readers' attention with an appealing layout, design, and illustrations. You've educated them with relevant information. You've aroused their interest and desire with persuasive copy. Now you have to let them know how to buy. The reader needs to see your company name, address, and phone number without having to hunt for them. Finally, you'll need a clear and visible call to action. (See Capturing Customers with Persuasive Words.)

Your piece has to get attention and clearly communicate information about your offer. Most important, it gives your customer a reason to buy!

Note that this full-color trade journal ad for Ad Systems includes all six of the features noted in the chapter.

Design Solutions For Specific Projects

Whatever your product, its packaging needs to say, *"Look at me. Pick me up. Buy my ideas."* In response, you want to hear your customers say, ***"Yes, I'm SOLD!"***

Every piece you create should incorporate eye-catching designs that sell. Generally, expert designers achieve this by:

- Using bold graphics and colors
- Using images that give them a personality
- Creating simple, elegant designs without clutter

Read on to see ways you can enhance both design and copy elements in a variety of situations.

In this section, you'll learn more about:

- **10 questions to answer before designing your flyer**
- **What makes a flyer a "must-have" marketing tool?**
- **A client-capturing website builds your brand *and* your bottom line**
- **Creating presentations that wow audiences**
- **Tips for designing book covers and inside pages**

10 Questions to Answer Before Designing Your Flyer

Before designing a flyer for an upcoming event, product announcement, or new service, answer the following questions:

1. What is your objective for this flyer?
2. To whom will it be going?
3. How will it be distributed?
4. Once your prospects have this flyer in hand, what action do you want them to take?
5. What benefits and key persuasive words will you use to get that result?
6. How will you create a sense of urgency in your wording?
7. Will you include photos? If so, color or black and white?
8. How will you design this flyer to have an image consistent with your other marketing pieces (same font, logo, tag line, etc.)?
9. What color and weight of paper will you use?
10. What size, shape, and fold will you use? Does the flyer need to be designed to fit in an envelope for mailing?

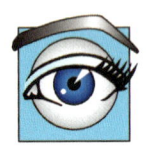

Eye-Popping Tip. *Keep the wording on your flyer simple by using a bullet style rather than a paragraph style. Use white space for easy readability. Select no more than two fonts. Make the overall look match your graphic identity package.*

© 2005 by Julie Wassom, 303-693-2306, www.juliewassom.com. All rights reserved, used by permission.

Design Solutions For Specific Projects

What Makes a Flyer A "Must-Have" Marketing Tool?

You meet someone who could hire you for your expertise and services. In the spirit of getting to know you, that decision-maker asks, "What do you speak about?" or "How do you help organizations?" or "Which groups have you worked with?"

Front side of Doug Butler's marketing flyer.

These questions become your opening to convey how you assist people and why you're the one experienced to do so. That's exactly what a marketing flyer does, too. To convey that you're a "must-have" expert, your flyer needs to be written and designed effectively.

Answers Key Questions

Your flyer, in effect, succinctly answers these seven questions that decision-makers would ask you in person at a first meeting:

1. How would you describe your area of expertise?

2. Whom do you work with and give presentations to?

3. What are the benefits of hiring you—

    - for the leaders of the organization?

    - for the participants in the ranks?

    - for organizational progress?

67

Turn Eye Appeal into Buy Appeal

Back side of Doug Butler's marketing flyer.

Visit www.macgraphics.net to see more sample flyers

4. What have you done that makes you an expert?

5. Which groups have you worked with before?

6. What did participants think of your contribution?

7. How can you be reached for more information?

Well-crafted words on your flyer answer these questions in the form of seven corresponding "must-have" elements:

1. Topics/Programs

2. Target Audience

3. Benefits (especially in headlines)

4. Biography

5. Client List

6. Testimonials

7. Contact Information

Adding Personality

Even if you have all of these elements in place, what turns it into a stronger "must-have" piece that represents you? In a word: *Personality.*

For example, Doug Butler's marketing flyer features these basics with lots of showmanship. Its overall look reflects the "personality" that participants want from him, achieving that appeal through these special graphic effects:

- 4-color photos of Doug portraying his Cowboy Wisdom theme.

- Graphics of cowboy symbols: a guitar, a horse, a lasso, a badge, a cowboy figure wearing a hat, bandana, and chaps—even a spurred cowboy boot.

- Cowboy Code message that stands out on the page.

- Benefits in the headlines: e.g., Bringing cowboy wisdom into the 21st century.

- Bio framed by a color photo that adds credibility for his message.

- List of target audiences, a sampling of clients, and comments from them.

- Well-designed company logo and easy-to-find contact info.

- NSA logo to show affiliation with a group recognized by decision-makers.

- Tag line: *"Forge a firm foundation with Doug's tried-and-true Cowboy Code."*

Through these words, themes, and graphics, Doug extends his warm personality to additional marketing pieces—his website, business card, handout materials, and so on. Together, they create a "must-have" look that appeals to decision-makers in organizations he wants to reach.

Thanks to writer/editor Barbara McNichol, www.BarbaraMcNichol.com, for her assistance in writing this chapter.

A Client-Capturing Website Builds Your Brand *and* Your Bottom Line

Website branding expert Kendall SummerHawk of KendallSummerHawk.com uses these five tips to create client-capturing website copy.

It's not enough for a website to describe what you do. Your website has to evoke emotion, build a sense of connection with your site visitor, and brand you as remarkable. A web brochure may be pretty but contributes little—if anything—to your bottom line.

The best—or bust: Your website as a revenue generator

Sadly, many websites languish, never fulfilling their promise. You should have higher expectations for your website! A client-capturing website uses design and compelling copy to grab your prospective clients' attention, tug on their heart, and inspire them to feel their problem can be solved—by you! A client-capturing website builds your bottom line by:

- Creating a remarkable brand identity for your business, putting you ahead of the competition.

- Shortening your sales cycle so you spend less time selling and more time focused on growing your business.

- Motivating prospective clients to contact you—making your marketing simple and easy.

- Weeding out the wrong kind of clients, leaving only the best for you to work with.

- Increasing your revenue, adding profit and value to your business.

5 Tips For Writing Client-Capturing Website Copy
Tip #1 Skip writing the headline until the very end.

It may seem counter-intuitive, but if you wait to write the headline, it will flow effortlessly. Focus instead on drafting—and crafting—a written conversation with your reader. When your draft is complete, take a look at the theme, or thread, running through it. Use the theme to craft a headline that clearly says what solution you offer and who is best helped by your coaching.

Design Solutions For Specific Projects

Tip #2 Ditch writing in vague, airy, general terms.

No matter what type of business you specialize in, capitalize on the opportunity to write about the specific situations and people you work best with. This will make your reader feel you know them, understand them, and can help them.

Tip #3 When you're not sure what to write, get up and walk around.

Staring at a blank screen or re-writing the same sentence umpteen times doesn't work. If you get stuck, get moving. Walk around your office or go outside for a couple of minutes. You'll find an idea will pop in to your head when you least expect it.

Tip #4 Always end each page with a clear call to action.

As a reader, I yearn to know why I should take action. Don't leave me puzzled about what to do next. One of my favorite ways to start a call to action is with the words, "It's your turn for/to . . . (fill in the blanks)."

Tip #5 Write for their hearts and their minds will follow.

Your message must be emotionally persuasive. It must touch your readers' hearts—or give them a kick in the pants. Either way, using juicy words will add spirit and style to your writing.

© 2005 by Kendall SummerHawk. All rights reserved. Used by permission.

The home page of Kendall SummerHawk is a great example of high-energy writing and crisp verbs used to create a strong, compelling emotional response. Visit www.KendallSummerHawk.com to read the text.

Turn Eye Appeal into Buy Appeal

Creating Presentations That Wow Audiences

Studies have shown that presentations using computer graphics (commonly called PowerPoint presentations) are 43% more persuasive than unaided presentations. Presenters were "perceived as significantly better prepared, more professional, more credible and more interesting" than those who use words only.

With today's technology, you can prepare a professional-looking presentation right on your desktop or laptop computer using popular software packages such as Microsoft PowerPoint or Apple Keynote. But once you've learned to use the software, what do you need to know to make your presentations "wow" your audiences? Here are great tips to keep in mind.

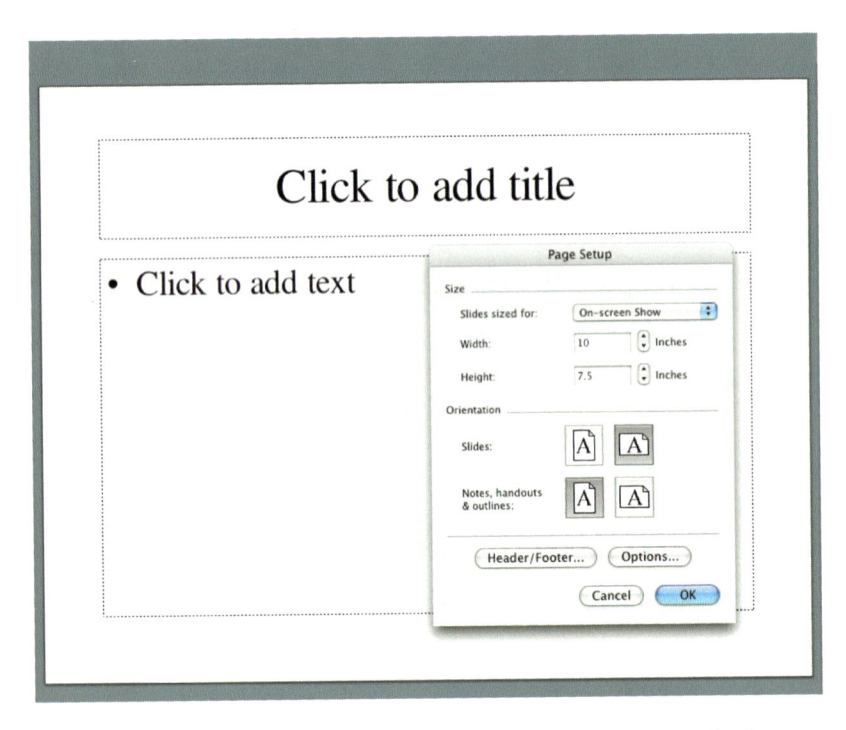

Choose Your Medium of Delivery

Use overheads for smaller groups where more interaction takes place between you and your audience or in rooms where the lights need to be on for note taking. On-screen slide shows work well for larger audiences.

For PowerPoint presentations, you'll need your laptop and a display device to project your computer presentation onto a large screen. Be sure the room you are presenting in can be made dark; bright lights or light from windows will wash out your projected images.

Select the correct size for your presentation. An on-screen slide show has a slightly different aspect ratio than 35mm slides. This information is in the "Page Setup" dialog box.

Design Solutions For Specific Projects

5 Steps for Preparing Your Visual Presentation

1. **Know your audiences.** Research their level of interest, knowledge, and experience with your subject. Anticipate their questions and build answers into your presentation. Target your message to the level and needs of your audience members.

2. **Organize your ideas into an outline.** Start by breaking down the major subject into subordinate topics and then organize the topics into the order you'll be discussing them. Generally you will create a slide for each topic or subtopic, depending on the complexity of your material.

3. **Make sure your slides are easy to read.** A good rule of thumb is to limit each slide to seven lines of text, with no more than seven words per line. Too much text will make your slides look crowded and the focus will be lost.

4. **Fit your content to a consistent format.** Use templates and master slides supplied by the software presentation package or your corporate communications department, or hire a designer to create a custom format based on your image, brand, or corporate identity. The format should be clean and simple.

5. **Choose contrasting colors for your background and text.** You may select a pre-made color palette from within the software. Light text (yellow, white) looks best on dark backgrounds (blues, black, gray). Do not use dark text (i.e., black) on a blue background, even if it seems to show up nicely on your laptop. The laptop screen is much brighter than what your projected image will be, and the black text will disappear into the blue.

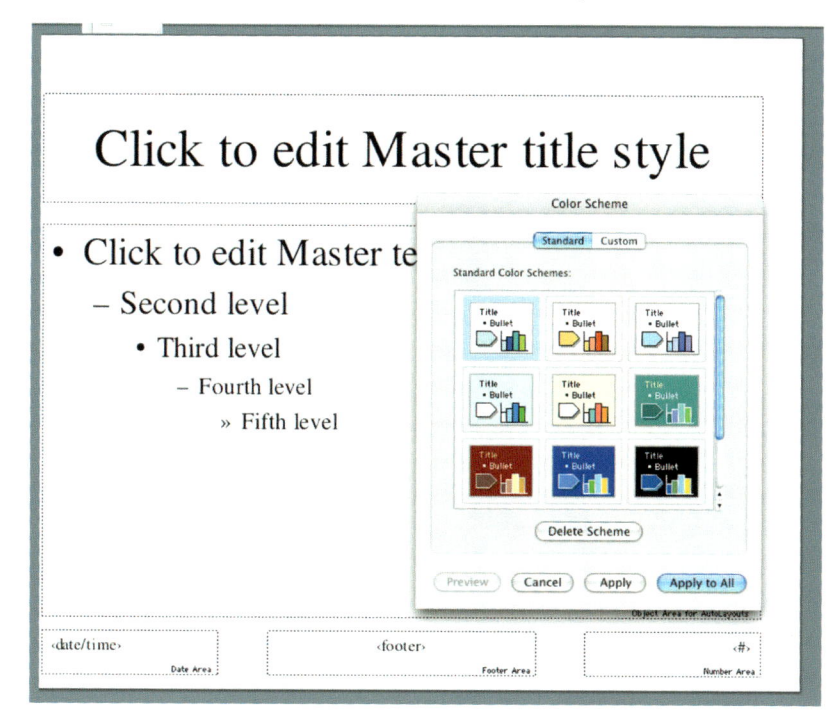

Use color schemes provided by your presentation software to select colors that will work well together.

73

Organize Your Presentation

- Create "opening" and "summary" slides. Keep your "overview" slide brief.

- Vary the flow of your presentation so that "text only" slides are interspersed with slides that have graphics. Break text-heavy slides into two or three frames.

- Use the slide sorter feature in your presentation software to move slides around.

- Print speaker notes for you and audience handouts for your audience. Capitalize on another marketing opportunity: Remember to include your contact information on the handouts.

Carefully Choose Your Fonts and Colors

- For an overhead presentation in normal light conditions, use dark type on a light background. For a slide presentation in a dark room, use light type on a dark background.

- Use short paragraphs and sentences; left justify your bullet points.

- Use large type and choose up to two fonts to use throughout the entire presentation. Use one font for the title, and the second font for the body text and bullets. Alternatively, you can use one font throughout the presentation with the titles in bold and body text and bullets in regular text.

- Use fonts that are of medium thickness and avoid thin or overly thick fonts. Your audience will find it easier to read Helvetica or Arial over a decorative font.

- Don't use all capital letters. Upper and lower case is much easier to read.

- Use one color for all the titles and a second color for all the text. All the bullets can be a third color. Use a different color on words you want to emphasize.

- "Paint up" your bullet points from the same direction on each slide. Paint up refers to how the slides transition from one to the other using, for example, a gradual fade or a wipe to the right.

Design Solutions For Specific Projects

About Graphics and Illustrations

1. Illustrate your presentation with charts, graphs, or graphics to help clarify points and hold audience attention.

    - Line graphs illustrate trends.

    - Bar charts clarify relationships between data.

    - Pie charts convey percentage relationships.

    - Flow charts and diagrams clear up complex concepts and ideas.

2. If you have a large chart or detailed data, provide it in a handout. Your audience will not be able to read the small print.

3. Keep the "style" of your graphics consistent. If you are using custom illustrations or clip art, use one source or one artist.

4. Illustrations help the audience make an association with a person, place, or product. But don't overload your presentation with graphics—use them when words alone don't tell the whole story.

5. Don't get too carried away with sound effects and animation. These gimmicks may distract your audience from the focus of your presentation if they are overused. Save them for those few times when added impact is necessary to make a point.

Eye-Popping Tip: *Be sure to practice giving your presentation with a timer. Meeting planners appreciate presenters who stick to their schedule precisely. Proofread your presentation carefully—and have others proofread it, too. Use key words and phrases and keep your presentation simple.*

Tips for Designing Book Covers and Inside Pages

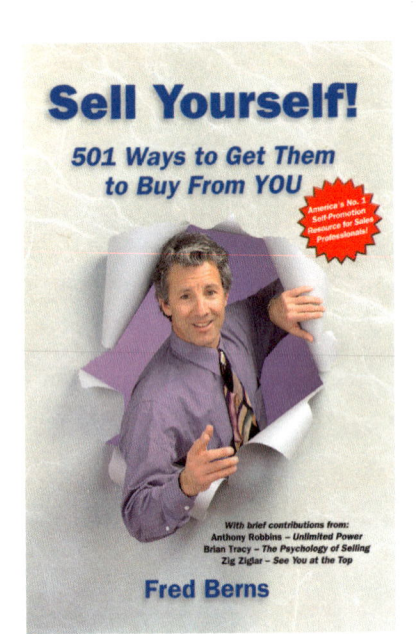

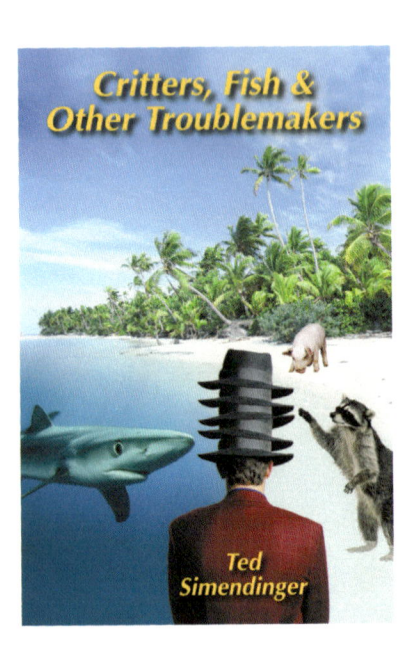

Keep in mind these elements when designing covers and interiors for your books, big and small.

Front Cover

The front cover presents your book title, subtitle, and your name. Golden opportunities often overlooked are including endorsements and short testimonials from VIPs.

I recommend using bold, contrasting lettering on the front cover. When choosing colors, consider how these colors will look when converted to black and white so your cover will reproduce well in black and white ads, catalogs, and flyers. Also make sure the font you use for the title is legible from a distance and appropriate for the book's subject.

Covers that scream "amateur" and have a "made-at-home look" make it difficult to sell your book at all. If you lack talent in this area, seek the services of an experienced book cover designer. A designer has the creativity, skills, software, access to stock photography, and printing knowledge that will make your cover stand out above others in the marketplace.

Spine

Your name, book title, and publishing company logo show up on the spine. Make sure the information on the spine is clean, uncluttered, and legible. I recommend using bold, contrasting lettering on the spine as well.

Back Cover

Place the category name in the upper left-hand corner to help bookstores shelve your book properly. Write a headline that clearly addresses who should buy the book. It should be followed by sales copy explaining what the book is about and bulleted items listing the benefits to readers.

Visit www.macgraphics.net to see more sample book covers.

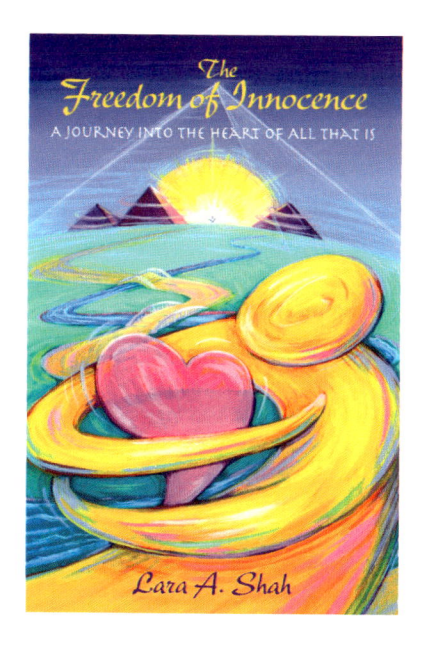

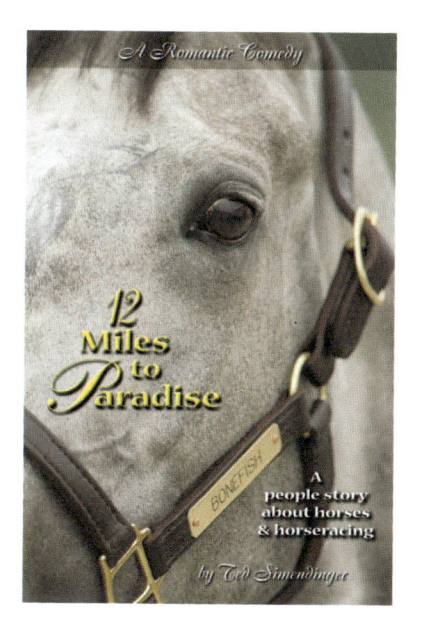

Design Solutions For Specific Projects

I recommend including no more than three testimonials and endorsements, as well as your bio and photograph. Close to the bottom, put "sales-closer" copy in bold print. Position the price in the lower left corner of the back cover. Also include the 13-digit ISBN number for cataloging and the bar code in the lower right corner (below ISBN number), which stores use for scanning information and price.

Don't forget to include credits for your book cover's illustrator, photographer, and/or designer.

Remember, book cover design is a form of packaging—and good packaging attracts buyers to products. That's why successful organizations spend millions researching and developing the best product packaging possible.

Inside Flaps (If Applicable)
- Sales copy
- Short "teaser" description of the book
- Your bio and photo

ISBN and Bar Code Requirements

The ISBN number identifies the publisher, title, author, and edition, and is used for ordering information for your book. Contact R.R. Bowker (800-521-8110). Order these in a series of 10 for $225. Retailers will need a bar code for sales transactions. You must know your ISBN number and retail price to obtain your bar code. You may order an electronic file of the bar code for $10–$30 and have it emailed to your designer. Note: UPC barcodes on books are being phased out. The current recommendation is to print only the Bookland EAN barcode on the back cover of publications (no more UPC). This transition has been approved as an international standard; it was started on January 1, 2005, and must be complete by January 1, 2007. Two companies that provide this service are Accugraphix (714-632-9000) and Bar-Code Graphics, Inc. (800-662-0701).

Another new policy requires you to convert a 10-digit ISBN (if you have one) into 13-digit ISBN starting with 978. All those affected by this change—organizations (publishers, distributors, retailers, librar-

*Visit **www.macgraphics.net** to see more sample book covers.*

ies, etc.) that record and exchange ISBN in automated systems—must ensure their systems can accommodate this ISBN-13 format. For more information, go to http://www.bisg.org/pi/index.html

Fonts for Inside Pages

First, read about typography in this guide. Then choose a font that appeals to you. Make sure it is appropriate for both the reader and the book. After all, fonts (like people) have personalities, and different designs will appeal to people of different ages. For example, if your readers are either very young or senior citizens, then choose a simple, well-designed font in a large size so the font can be read without strain. Set your column width to allow for at least a 1" to 1.25" gutter, and .5" border for top, bottom, and outside edges.

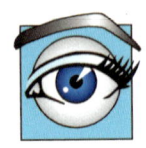

Eye-Popping Tip: *Don't use all caps for your heads, subheads or table of contents, because this style is difficult to read.*

Word Spacing

Proper word spacing creates greater legibility and is also more pleasing aesthetically. Make sure there is neither too much space nor too little space between words. Too much space creates vertical "rivers of white" coursing through the pages, and is often seen in newspapers where columns are very narrow.

Leading

Leading is the space between lines of type. Your choice of font, type size, word spacing, and length of line all affect the amount of leading you will need. Some visual judgment comes into play. (For more details, see Setting the Tone of Your Text with Tracking, Leading, and Line Length.)

Alignment

Most books are set full justified because this style best suits sustained reading comfort.

Length of Line (Column Width)

Reading many long lines of type causes fatigue. And lines that are too short break up words or phrases that are generally read as a unit. The length of line depends on the size of the type. A good rule of thumb is to set a line about 65 characters long.

Eye-Popping Tip: *Go to bookstores and peruse books in your category of interest. Take notes on the ones you find attractive and ask which ones are selling best. This will give you excellent clues about effective design.*

Paper Stock for Interior Pages

The typical paper used for book interiors is a 50# or 60# smooth offset stock in white. Natural or creme color is also popular, but usually is a little more expensive. A 50# white paper is less expensive than 60# white, but is also less opaque and less bulky. Opaque paper is less transparent and will keep you from seeing the printing on the back of each page. Use a bulkier paper or vellum stock to increase the spine width of a thin book. Vellum is not as smooth, but is bulkier than smooth offset stock. If you have photographs or screens, it is best to use a matte or gloss coated stock so that your photos will print with high definition. Most stock is now acid free, which keeps the paper from yellowing over the years. Make sure the book stock is printed with the correct grain direction to prevent the book from opening and closing uncomfortably.

Ask your printer for samples and pricing on "house stock." You'll get better pricing on house stock since the printer buys it in bulk on a regular basis.

Paper for Book Covers

The standard perfect bound book cover is 10 pt C1S (coated one side). Curl-free film laminate that comes in gloss or matte finish will protect the ink on the cover. UV (ultra violet), aqueous, and varnish can also be used to protect the cover but are not as durable as lamination. Dust jackets are usually printed on an 80# or 100# C1S. In a casebound book, the boards can be covered with a B grade cloth, leather, or paper and foil stamped. "Litho" (hard cover) books usually have an 80# C1S Litho paper laminated to a .88 pt. board.

Working With Digital Imagery

For most marketing pieces, you'll want to incorporate photos and scans that add buy appeal as well as eye appeal. In today's computer graphic terms, they're referred to as Digital Imagery.

This section addresses your technical concerns when creating the imagery you want in your documents.

In this section, you'll read more about:

- **Learning to work with digital photos**
- **What to consider when buying a scanner**
- **How to scan photos at the correct resolution**

Learning to Work with Digital Photos

The technology that goes into digital cameras has come a long way in the last few years. Models now come in all sizes with a variety of pixel depths, zoom lens, and media card capacities. But what does having these features mean when it comes to designing your marketing pieces? Simply this: It's easier than ever to fold digital photographs into your designs and boost the quality as well as the eye appeal.

If you're new to using digital prints, I recommend learning several "tricks" that will help you save and organize your digital photos. Here are some ideas.

Media Cards

As you take photos with your digital camera, you have the option of saving your image files to a "Compact Flash," a "SD," or a media card that is inside your camera. These cards are physically small, but can hold hundreds of images and can be purchased in various capacities. Remember, the higher the "megapixel" of your camera, the more storage space each photo will occupy on the media card. To transfer the files to your computer, you will need a special cable, disk drive, or card reader. These are available at stores where you buy digital cameras and computers.

Eye-Popping Tip. *If you take lots of photos, even the largest media card will become full, so keep an eye on how much you're filling the card.*

Organizing Your Images

Select and use a good image-organizing software to keep track of all your photos. For example, the OS X operating system on my Macintosh comes with iPhoto. PCs users can use PhotoDirector by Picasa or one of your favorite retail photo developer's software such as RitzPix E-Z Print and Share. These applications automate the process of copying images from your camera's media card to your computer.

Working With Digital Imagery

With this software, you can organize your images by "albums," delete the ones you don't want, view thumbnails (small versions of the photos shown several to a page), and even put together a slide show with music. It also allows you to attach albums or individual photos to emails, burn CDs, and do minor retouching. Most of these programs have a feature that lets you upload an entire album or individual images to a website so you can share images with your friends and order prints.

Pixel Depth and Cropping

Each digital camera has a specific maximum number of pixels that can be imaged. For example, my Pentax Optio S50 is specified as a "5.0 megapixel" camera. This means that 5 million pixels are available to be imaged onto one rectangular area.

Using my camera, for example, that means each photo would be 2650 pixels by 1920 pixels. This is a fairly high-resolution file and will average about 3.3 MB (megabytes) of space. I would be able to print up to a 16" x 20" enlargement print from this file without any "pixellation" (jaggy-looking, bitmapped images). However, if I crop the photo, I would be deleting pixels and therefore wouldn't be able to enlarge it much before pixilation occurs.

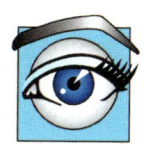

Screen shot of iPhoto (photo organization software from Apple)

Eye-Popping Tip: *The rectangular area in your camera's LCD monitor is* **not** *the same aspect ratio as a typical 4" x 6" print. About 1/4" at the top and bottom will be cropped off in the print. Keep this in mind when you frame your shot.*

83

Quick Reference Table

Megapixel Camera	Maximum Photo Enlargement Print	Maximum Photo Size in Offset Printed Document
3.0	8" x 10"	6.5" on longest side
4.0	10" x 16"	7.5" on longest side
5.0	16" x 20"	8.5" on longest side

JPG and TIF File Formats

All digital cameras save photo image files in the JPG file format, which is a compressed file format that loses quality every time the file is opened and closed. That's why I recommend copying all the files from your camera media card onto your computer. After doing that, you can open the file you want to work with and resave it in the TIF format with a different file name. It would be wise to give it a highly descriptive name and add the letters "edit" or "rev" (for revised) to the file name to differentiate it from the original file. Keep it in the TIF format until you are ready to image the print. Note: Some photo developers can work with the TIF format while others require it in JPG so you may have to convert it back to a JPG file.

Other File Formats and Specifications

If you plan to put the image on your website, I recommend you save it as a 72 PPI (pixels per inch), also referred to as DPI (dots per inch) JPG file; for your PowerPoint presentation, it should be saved as a 96 PPI JPG file.

If you want to print an image in a Microsoft Word or page layout program using a desktop inkjet printer, save your file as a 150 PPI TIF file. For offset printing, it needs to be a 300 PPI TIF file. You will also need to save your file in the proper color "space" or "system." (For more about color systems, see RGB and CMYK—Colorful but Different.)

Working With Digital Imagery

A snapshot of leaves . . .

. . . is transformed into a beautiful drawing by applying the "Pastel" filter in Photoshop.

Editing Your Photos

You'll want to edit your photos using a photo-editing software program such as Adobe Photoshop Elements or Photoshop CS. Using these programs, you can crop the photo, convert its format from JPG to TIF, convert colors from RGB to CMYK, adjust brightness and color contrast, fix problems such as red eye (when the subjects' eyes are red in the photo), and much more.

These programs feature cloning tools that allow you to touch up areas by picking up other areas and pasting them into the problem areas. For example, if you have a telephone pole sticking out from the back of your subject's head, just "clone" some of the blue sky over it and you can make that pole disappear.

In addition, photo-editing programs usually have filters to change the image to appear as if it was painted in watercolor, sketched in pastels, and other effects. By adding a little time and talent to your original image, you can make your photos look like artwork and add a lot of eye appeal.

Eye-Popping Tip. *Your last step in editing your photo is to "sharpen" its focus, giving it a crisp edge and giving you the sharp result you want.*

What to Consider When Buying a Scanner

How do you turn a drawing, painting or photographic print into a digital image you can use in your marketing pieces? You scan them, using a photocopy-like machine called a scanner.

Scanners are popular tools for doing desktop publishing and web design. You'll find a wide range of scanners available—from a low-cost black and white hand-held variety to high-quality, professional color devices. For the highest quality, printers and service bureaus use expensive drum scanners. The high-quality scans they produce are required for high-end printing projects such as book and magazine covers, images for coffee table books, and advertisements. A skilled operator using a CCD (charge-coupled device) flatbed scanner can produce similar high-quality scans.

Optical Resolution

When determining which scanner to use for your work, look for optical resolution specifications. These are two numbers that indicate how many pixels per inch (e.g., 600 x 600 PPI) are scanned in each direction. (I suggest you ignore the interpolated resolution numbers—these are measurements made when the scanner inserts new pixels between scanned ones.)

How much resolution your scan needs depends on how you plan to use your scanned images. For example, photos for offset printing are usually scanned at 300 PPI. Line art (such as black and white pen and ink illustrations) for offset printing need to be scanned at 1200 PPI to ensure that the lines are smooth. Images to be printed on desktop laser or color inkjet printers are scanned at 100 to 200 PPI. Photos and line art for the Internet are scanned at 72 PPI while images for PC-PowerPoint presentations are 96 PPI. Text that will be converted to text characters (using OCR technology) are scanned at 300 to 400 PPI.

Working With Digital Imagery

Eye-Popping Tip. *Always scan your images at the final size you plan to use them. Do not enlarge your scans, as they will lose resolution.*

Dynamic Range

Most flatbed scanners have a dynamic range of about 2.4. If you need to display better detail in shadow areas or you plan to scan negatives and slides, you may be better off using a top-quality color flatbed or drum scanner that can provide a dynamic range of 2.8 to 3.2.

Bit Depth

Most color scanners are at least 24-bit, which results in near-photographic quality in terms of the range of colors. Scanners that are 30-bit and 36-bit can capture billions of colors. I recommend these for scanning slides and negatives, but beware that few software packages can open these files. Note: Not all monitors can display 24-bit color. If you're using an 8-bit (256-color) monitor, then a 24-bit image may look blotchy on screen.

Other Consideations

In general, CCD (charge-coupled devices) produce better scans than low profile, less expensive scanners. Make sure the scanning bed is large enough for your documents. Consider the scanner's speed and determine if you need a slide adapter. Sheetfed scanners take up less room on your desktop, but you can't scan a 3-D object or book using this kind of scanner.

An option that may come with a scanner and affect its cost is software. Yes, you will need to have photo-editing software (such as Adobe Photoshop) to create quality scans, especially from less-than-perfect originals.

To connect your scanner to your computer, determine what type of connection your computer can support: parallel port, SCSI port, or USB port. Ask the experts where you buy your computer equipment if you are in doubt.

Eye-Popping Tip: *OCR (optical character recognition) software allows a scanner to read handwritten or printed text, then convert it into text characters that can be read by any word processing software. OmniPage and Text Bridge are examples of two OCR software programs.*

Turn Eye Appeal into Buy Appeal

How to Scan Photos at the Correct Resolution

An extremely important element in getting the best results from your desktop scanner is understanding how to get good resolution from your photos. Let me explain the basics.

Halftones and Lines per Inch (LPI)

In graphics arts terminology, a photograph from your camera is called a "continuous tone" image. Printing presses require a continuous tone image to be converted into a "halftone." A halftone is created by placing a "screen" made of thousands of dots on the photo and taking a "picture" of it.

Nowadays, this screening process happens using computer software. The screens vary in density and the resolution is measured in lines per inch or LPI. This term refers to the number of dots that the screen places on the photo for every linear inch. The higher the LPI, the smoother the shades look.

Pixels Per Inch (PPI)

Pixels per inch is a unit of measure for scanned images. For example, one photo scanned at a higher PPI than another will have more pixels and the pixels will be smaller. This combination results in getting a better resolution and therefore a higher quality of photo.

Scanning Resolution for Print Images

The resolution you need to scan your photo depends on the size of the original image, the size you want to reproduce it to, and the output method or device you're using. Your printed output choices include laser, inkjet, digital and offset printing.

I recommend that you scan your photo so that the number of pixels per inch (PPI) at output size is two times the number of lines per inch (LPI). For example, if you are scanning a photo for an offset printing press, your printer may tell you the photo will be screened at 150 LPI. Based on this information, you will need to scan your photo at 300 PPI. If you scan an image at too low a resolution, it may show pixellation, often referred to as "bitmapping."

A photo scanned at 300 PPI

A photo scanned at a very low resolution will show pixellation.

Working With Digital Imagery

Eye-Popping Tip. *Another reason to scan your photo at the final size and not enlarge it is because enlarging it will require a higher PPI in direct relation to the amount of enlargement. It would be considered overkill to scan your photo higher than two times the LPI because the PostScript software can't use the larger file. In addition, it will take a longer time to download and process.*

Scanning Resolution for Website Images

Unlike printed output, websites do not have LPI requirements. Still, I recommend you always scan a photo being used on the Internet at the actual size you intend to display it. To prevent having photos that take a long time to download when accessing your website, I suggest you do not scan your photos at a resolution that's higher than 72 PPI.

Scanning Photos from Already Printed Sources

Avoid scanning a photo that has already been printed because it has already been "screened" (converted to halftone). If you do, you won't like the blotchy results you'll get.

Scanning Specifications

Refer to the chart below for recommended scanning resolutions.

Output	Typical LPI*	Resolution (PPI)
Laser printer	50-75	100-150
Newspaper	85-100	170-200
Glossy, coated magazine	150-200	300-400
Uncoated paper (newsletters, stationery, book interiors)	133-150	266-300
Websites	Not Applicable**	72

* Always ask your printer for the specific LPI
** Websites do not have LPI requirements

The Role Of Color In Your Design

Even though printing your marketing pieces in color increases the expense, it adds considerable impact that you won't want to forego.

You'll gain a more informed opinion about using color after reading the chapters in this section.

In this section, you'll learn about:

- **How color can add "zing" to your design**
- **Easy ways to select harmonious colors**
- **Unlocking the symbolic meaning of color**
- **RGB and CMYK—colorful but different**
- **Making monitor colors match your printed piece**

How Color Can Add "Zing" to Your Design

Vibrant colors add an exciting dimension to your marketing materials, but no one has to tell you 4-color graphics cost a lot more to print than black and white or 2-color graphics. How do you determine when it's cost effective to go the distance and get full color?

In my experience, items such as book covers and video/audio/CD packages need to sell themselves on appearance alone. Often impulse buys, these items merit vibrant colors and attention-grabbing graphics or they fade away on the sellers' shelves. By a phenomenally higher percentage, buyers are more likely to purchase books with a professionally designed, full-color cover than with an amateur cover that has only one or two colors.

For author Lin McNeil, I designed the second edition of her *7 Keys* book cover using fresh graphics and full-color printing. Notice how the full-color cover jumps off the page compared with the original two-color version.

Original book in 2-color *Full-color book cover*

The Role Of Color In Your Design

When a portrait makes up the central graphic element in your piece, you want it to evoke a warm, personable feeling from the natural flesh tones of a full-color original photo. Add to that a colorful garment and action pose. Together, these color elements draw attention to the photo, which is what you want!

In Diane Sieg's flyer, notice how her personality comes alive with the use of full color. As a result, the most important graphic element—her colorful fun portrait—becomes the focal point of the page.

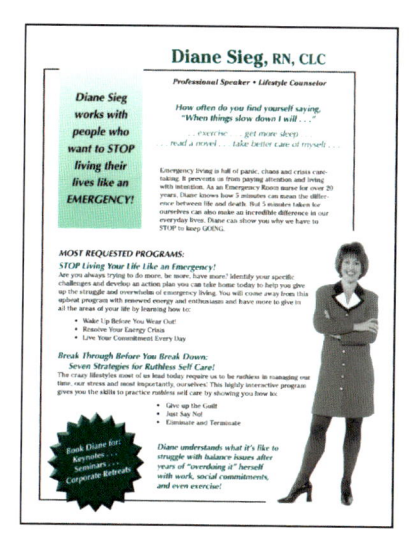

I recommend cutting back to 2-color graphics for your printed stationery and newsletters. That way, you can save your money for full-color printing on projects that demand more pizzazz—those have to jump off the sellers' shelves.

Eye-Popping Tip: *Printing full-color graphics on a traditional offset press becomes cost-effective in quantities above 1000. In many cases, a quantity of 500 usually costs only $30 less than a 1000. Why? Because the printer's set-up charges make up most of the initial cost.*

Want an alternative to offset printing? Consider opting for digital printing or color copies for quantities below 500. Color copies are priced per page without an initial set-up charge. Do your research and determine where the price break is for the quantity you want to print. That will help you decide which option to choose. (For more information on printing options, see What's the Difference Between a Digital and Offset Printer?)

Easy Ways to Select Harmonious Colors

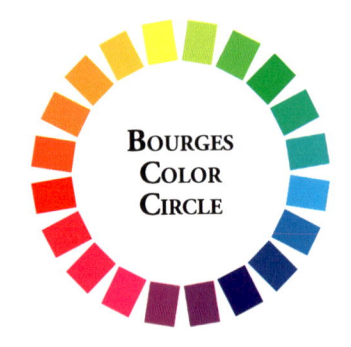

You experience harmonious colors in many areas of life: clothing, architecture, interior design, jewelry, gardening, as well as advertising, marketing, and corporate identity.

It becomes easy to select harmonious colors if you follow a proven color theory system. The steps below will show you how to create well-planned color schemes based on the "Bourges color circle" system. (See the diagram on the left.) Albert Bourges based his color theory on a circle of 20 hues.

Complementary Colors

Complementary colors are exact opposites that enhance one another. When you blend the two together, you get neutral black. When used together, they both appear brighter and more exciting. To find complementary colors, just draw a line through the circle from a hue on one side to the hue on the exact opposite side of the circle.

M. E. Chevreul discovered that complementary colors create an unusual optical illusion. Stare at a color for several seconds, then shut your eyes. Open them, and look at a white sheet of paper. Immediately an image of the color's complement will appear!

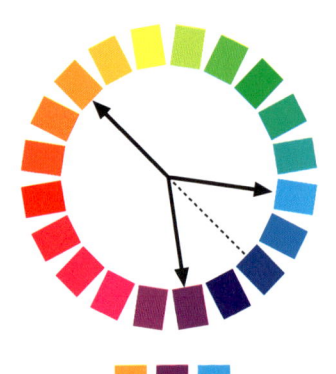

Split Complements

If you would like a palette of three colors, first find the true complement of your chosen color; then move one, two or three more spaces away on either side. A split complementary color scheme is usually more pleasing than a true complementary scheme. (Refer to the diagram on the left.)

The Role Of Color In Your Design

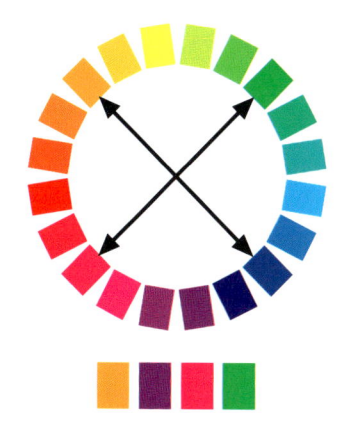

Four Color Harmony

To create a color scheme consisting of four colors, first select a color and its complement, then draw a perpendicular line across the circle so that your lines resemble a cross. (Refer to the diagram on the left.)

This will create a balanced palette of two sets of complements and two related pairs of colors.

Select one of these four hues as your main theme color, then use a small amount of the other three hues to enhance it. You may include darker or lighter shades of these four colors for more variety.

For more information about the Bourges color circle and the science of color, see Color Bytes *by Jean Bourges.*

95

Unlocking the Symbolic Meaning of Color

Color is a magical element that gives feeling and emotion to art, design, and advertising. By understanding the symbolic meaning of different colors, you can choose the right color to support and emphasize your design.

A dominant color or overall color scheme can determine the tone of your document. Certain colors will help your product, corporate document, or advertisement attract specific audiences and evoke desired responses.

The information below provides generally accepted guidelines on the symbolic meanings of color and how you can use color more effectively in your marketing pieces.

Yellows — Coral, orange, amber, gold

Symbolizes: Energy, caution, warmth, cheer, joy

Yellows are often associated with the following characteristics: homey, friendly, soft, welcoming, moving, excitement, or adventure. Good for press kits, stationery, and shopping bags.

Use yellow for signage in work situations warning of danger. Yellow is also good for any project that needs to evoke feelings of lightheartedness, humor, or friendliness.

Reds — Mauve, magenta, crimson, scarlet, poster red

Symbolizes: Power, romance, vitality, earthly, energy

Reds evoke highly charged emotions such as aggression, danger, or love. Red makes us pay attention and catches our eye immediately so use reds on items that need to grab attention.

In the financial arena, red symbolizes a negative direction.

Greens — Lime, leaf green, sea green, emerald, teal, sage

Symbolizes: life, foliage, grass, trees, water

Greens are sensuous and alive. Green is associated with the following characteristics: friendliness, dependability, freshness, non-threatening, safe, secure, healthy, strong, expensive, and primitive.

In the business world, green symbolizes growth and prosperity.

Blues — Cyan, sky blue, ultramarine, violet, purple, azure

Symbolizes: Peace, law and order, logic, analytical, intelligent, honest, calm, clean, good will, tranquility, compassionate, serious, thoughtful, quiet, reflective, regal, classic, dependable, trustworthiness, tradition, magical.

Blues are often used for older, more mature audiences and situations. Blue is common in financial institutions, hospitals, and legal and medical professions. Purples have long been associated with magic, royalty, nobility and spirituality.

Eye-Popping Tip: *When you learn how to use color as a functional design element, you'll love the results.*

RGB and CMYK—
Colorful but Different

Are you confused by what these two acronyms mean? Do you know how they affect your desktop publishing and website files? These letters represent two different color systems, which are types of color definitions.

Red, Green, and Blue (RGB)

RGB stands for Red, Green, and Blue, with the first letter of each word represented in the acronym. RGB is called an "additive color" system.

Red, green, and blue beams of light create the colorful images on your computer monitor; where red and green light overlap, you see yellow; where red, green, and blue mix together, you see white. (See the diagram on the left.) The same is true for devices that electronically display or record color, such as televisions, scanners, digital cameras, cell phones, and personal digital assistants.

I recommend saving your graphics files in the RGB format for these uses: websites, CD ROM development, animation, video capture, and scanning.

Cyan, Magenta, Yellow, and Black (CMYK)

The CMYK color system works in the opposite fashion to RGB. CMY stands for Cyan, Magenta, Yellow, and the K stands for black. CMYK are color pigments or inks used in the printing industry. This color arrangement is known as "subtractive color."

The combination of CMY inks creates gray. Black is added to deepen the shadows and to print solid black areas. Your files need to be converted into CMYK before a printer will be able to put your job on a press.

RGB Color Model—Combination of RGB light beams produces white.

CMYK Color Model—Uses subtractive color plus black.

The Role Of Color In Your Design

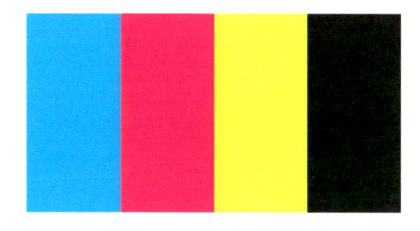

Cyan - Magenta - Yellow - Black

The "K" in black is often misunderstood to be named after the K for the last letter in the word black. Actually, it is named after "keyline," which was the press plate that carried the text copy or keyline information and was always printed in black.

When you look at a color printed piece, (such as a magazine) the millions of colors that you "see" are actually made of only four colors of ink! For fun, take a magnifying glass to examine a magazine closely. You will see thousands of tiny dots of cyan, magenta, yellow, and black ink, which make small rosette patterns.

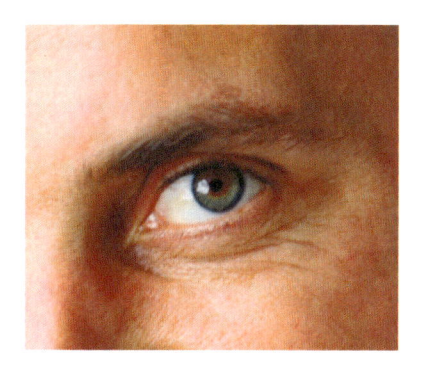

Eye of a model as seen in a printed piece.

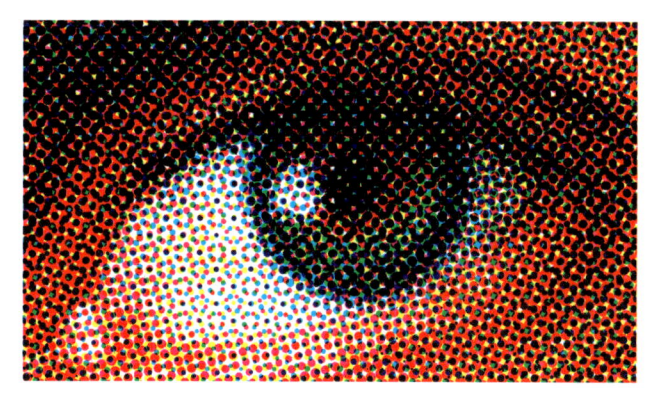

Eye of the model magnified to see the rosette pattern made up of tiny CMYK dots.

Making Monitor Colors Match Your Printed Piece

Have you been frustrated when the colors displayed on your monitor don't match the colors of your final printed documents? Not using a calibrated monitor can lead to mistakes, printing delays, or reprinted jobs—all of which cost time and money.

This problem happens because most monitors display many more colors than most printing processes, and the majority of monitors are not calibrated properly.

International Color Consortium

A group of industry professionals founded the International Color Consortium® (ICC) to tackle this issue. The ICC developed a way to translate and standardize colors across computer platforms (Windows, Macintosh, UNIX); affecting graphic programs, monitors, scanners, digital cameras, and printing equipment. They developed a process that uses "ICC profiles," a key part of color management.

ICC profiles are files that provide a way to ensure consistent color. These files are specific to each device on your system and contain information about how that device produces color. The graphic file displayed on your monitor is assigned a specific ICC profile that will simulate the colors on the color proofing system and on the printing press. The result—what you see on your monitor is what you will get when it is printed!

Where Do You Get ICC Profiles?

More and more printers are adopting this technology and have ICC profiles ready for use. Be sure to ask them if they have an ICC profile of their proofing system or printing press. (You will need an ICC profile from every printing company you work with because printers use different equipment and software).

The Role Of Color In Your Design

With color management installed, the color on your monitor will simulate . . .

. . . the color on your proof prints . . .

. . . and the color on your offset printed job.

Color Management System

What else do you need to do to set up your office with a color management system (CMS)?

You'll need to calibrate your monitor and create a monitor profile. You have a choice of using high-end software with a suction-cup device (spectrophotometer), or doing the calibration visually with software such as Color Sync Default Calibrator or Adobe Gamma. Or, you may want to hire a prepress specialist to do the installation and calibration for you.

Make sure you stabilize the light sources in your office to minimize any change in ambient light. Warm daylight and cool tungsten lamps will make your images look different on your monitor. It is also a good idea to set your desktop (computer "wallpaper" or background color) to a neutral gray.

Thanks to Bill Owen for his contribution to this chapter.

Getting Graphics Files Ready To Print

You're happy with your design; you're ready to get your "baby" off your desktop and into the hands of the printer. But are you sure that you're completely ready?

This section helps you make sure you've prepared your documents properly so the printer can do a good job without requiring time-consuming (and costly) changes to the files you've created.

In this section, you'll learn about:

- **Proper file formats for Internet and print**
- **The versatility of PDF files**
- **Checklist for making your files print-ready**

Turn Eye Appeal into Buy Appeal

Proper File Formats for Internet and Print

Using the proper file format and resolution for the job can mean the difference between a professional-looking document and one that looks blurry or is missing graphics. Graphic file formats for the Internet and offset printing are totally different animals. Do not interchange them!

Graphics for the Internet

Low-resolution raster graphics are used on the Internet. These graphics are made up of thousands of pixels (squares of color). Internet browsers will read JPG and GIF graphics, which are best scanned or sized at 72 PPI (pixels per inch). Because of the limits of screen resolution, anything greater will result in larger file sizes and longer download times than necessary. All Internet graphics are limited to a special palette of 256 colors.

Scan your photos using RGB colors to the JPG file format. JPG file sizes are very small and compatible with nearly every graphical browser. This format is best suited for photographs and any image that contains a complex mixture of colors.

The GIF format is best suited for images with a limited number of distinct colors and graphics that have sharp, distinct edges (most logos, menus and buttons). A special GIF89a file format gives you the option to make the background transparent so you don't get a white rectangle behind the graphic.

Graphics for Offset Printing

Graphics for offset printing require much higher resolution than for websites. If you use a low-resolution graphic (i.e., a logo copied from a website) on an offset printed job, a fuzzy "bitmapped" image—or no image—will result.

Offset printed graphics can be one of two types: Vector-based or high-resolution raster. Raster images (which are color or grayscale digital photos and scans) must be at least 300 PPI (pixels per inch) and in the TIF (Tagged Image File) or EPS (Encapsulated PostScript)

72 PPI JPG photo for the Internet. Note the large pixels.

The graphic used on this page is for simulation purposes only.

Getting Graphic Files Ready To Print

file format. Your scans of black and white line art (images that do not contain any shades of gray) must be at least 1200 PPI. Be careful not to enlarge your raster graphics, because the pixels will also enlarge and become more noticeable. (For more information on scanning resolutions, see How to Scan Photos at the Correct Resolution.)

Vector-based graphics are made of mathematically defined lines and curves. Because they are not made of pixels, these unique files can be scaled to any size without losing their crisp, smooth edges. Use professional drawing programs such as Adobe Illustrator, Macromedia Freehand, or Corel Draw to create these types of graphics for printing, saving them in the EPS format.

Color Ink Systems for Printing

Color files for offset printing must be specified with PMS or CMYK inks. Do not use RGB colors unless you are planning to print *only* to a low-end color desktop printer. (For more information on RGB color uses, see RGB and CMYK—Colorful But Different. For a description of PMS—Pantone Matching System—inks, see How Can You Maximize Two-Color Printing.)

300 PPI TIF photo for offset printing.

A vector-based graphic has no pixels.

The graphics used on this page are for simulation purposes only.

105

The Versatility of PDF Files

A PDF (Portable Document Format) file is the most reliable, efficient way to share documents across platforms—Windows, Macintosh, or UNIX. The layout, content, fonts, and graphics in your file are preserved and can be viewed and printed. Adobe Acrobat is one of several software applications that can convert just about any type of file into the PDF format. To view and print PDF files, you will need the free Adobe Acrobat "Reader" software, available at www.adobe.com .

Universal File Format

A PDF file can be "optimized for the web" at low resolution and serve as an online form, a downloadable book or document, or a proof in the review process. It can be "optimized for print" at medium resolution for printing on desktop inkjet and laser printers. The plug-in called "PDF Writer," included in Microsoft Word 2000 for Windows program, is a limited version of Acrobat Distiller and can create low-resolution PDF files.

To create high-resolution PDF files for offset printing, you will need to purchase the Adobe Acrobat software program that includes the "Distiller" module for approximately $250. This software will create PDF files that are "optimized for the press." Many printing companies accept PDF files. This is very helpful when the printer does not support the program in which you created your project.

Professional Page Layout Programs vs. Word Processing Programs

Professional page layout programs such as Adobe PageMaker, In-Design, and Quark Xpress are designed for creating documents for offset printing. They have the capability to handle fonts, graphics, color separations, and other essential pre-press operations. By contrast, word processing programs such as Microsoft Word are designed to perform in the office setting and fall short in providing the pre-press features. However, you can use Adobe Acrobat software to convert *black and white* Microsoft Word files into press-compatible PDF files. At this time, you cannot create a *high* resolution PDF file from a *color* Microsoft Word document.

Creating a PDF File for Offset Printing

Before you create a PDF file, you will first need to create a PostScript file, using your printer driver. This will embed the fonts and graphics into the PostScript or EPS file. Then, ask your printing company for their PDF file settings or get their "job options" file. Place this tiny file into the Distiller "settings" folder. It has all your printer's technical specifications for printing the job at his/her plant. Print a final proof from your PDF file to check for possible missing fonts and other errors. Send this proof with your PDF file to your printer. Be aware that some printers may charge a fee to fix your file or add a surcharge for PDF files made from Microsoft Word documents.

Eye-Popping Tip: *Be sure to consult with your printing company to get specific PDF file settings and avoid any problems on press.*

Helpful Tips for High-Resolution PDF Files

If you have imported graphics, be sure your photos are 300 PPI and in the TIF or EPS file format. All line art needs to be 1200 PPI. Don't use the "style palette" to create fonts that you don't have (i.e., if you have the Times font, but not the Times Bold font, don't make your font simulate Times Bold by choosing the "Bold" in the style palette). Stay with black and white for text and graphics if you are doing your page layout in Microsoft Word. Use a professional page layout program to make *color* files for offset printing. Use the Adobe Reader software to view your PDF files before you send them to your printer.

Research printing companies to find one that you are comfortable with and that has good technical support for creating PDF files. Go to www.Adobe.com to download the free Acrobat Reader or to purchase the full program. Also, you'll find the following Internet resources helpful for making PDF files.

http://www.planetpdf.com/mainpage.asp?webpageid=1903
(A tutorial on creating PDFs)

http://www.planetpdf.com/mainpage.asp?webpageid=1519&nl
(Advice for creating PDFs)

Checklist for Making Your Files Print-Ready

Following this checklist will help you determine if your files are completely ready to send to the printer.

Fonts

- Make sure all your fonts are included on the disc. Include both the printer and screen versions of PostScript fonts.

- If you are submitting a PDF file, make sure you've embedded all fonts and images.

Graphics

- Include all your image files on the disc. (Image files are scans, photos, logos, graphics, etc., that are created in a separate drawing or photo-editing program then "inserted" into your page layout program.)

- Convert all RGB graphics to CMYK, grayscale, or PMS and all photos to CMYK or grayscale.

- Convert all graphics and photos to the TIF or EPS format. An exception: The Adobe CS Suite programs can use native files.

- Make sure all your graphics are high resolution: 300 PPI (pixels per inch) for halftones and 1200 PPI for line art.

- Make sure you include at least 1/8" bleed on all items that print to the edge of the page. That is, extend your image area 1/8" beyond the trim size.

- Spell ink color names exactly the same in all applications where they are used.

Proofs

- Include the most current hard copy with the package you send to the printer.

- Get a high-resolution color proof of all pages before you print your job. Your printer or a pre-press vendor can supply this color proof.

Convert B&W photos to grayscale and save at 300 PPI.

Convert RGB color photos to CMYK and save at 300 PPI.

Getting Graphic Files Ready To Print

Color graphics should be spot color (usually PMS) or CMYK, never RGB.

- Make sure your document "page size" matches the trim size specified in the price quotation from the printing company.

- If you make a PDF file, distill the PostScript file using the settings provided by your printing company. You can probably request a special "job options" file from your printer to automate this process.

- Complete and enclose your printer's "Electronic File Submissions" form.

- Get your printer's list of accepted applications and their corresponding version numbers. Check to make sure you've designed your job within these parameters. Make changes if necessary.

Eye-Popping Tip: *Before you submit your next job to your printing company, check the items on this list first. This is **not** a complete and thorough list, but it does contain some of the most common problems printing companies have when they receive computer graphics files.*

Answers To Your Printing Questions

Answers to these frequently asked questions become your guidelines for choosing and working with the right printer and the correct printing specifications for your project.

In this section, you'll learn answers to these questions:

- **What should you consider when choosing a printer?**
- **What's the difference between a digital and offset printer?**
- **How can you save money on color printing?**
- **How can you maximize two-color printing?**
- **What paper works best?**
- **What special effects will add flair to your print job?**
- **What kind of folding do you need?**
- **What are your options for binding?**

What Should You Consider When Choosing a Printer?

Different types of printing companies specialize in different types of printing including offset or traditional printing, digital printing, book printing, gang printing, print on demand, web press for extremely high quantities, and so on.

You have a number of options to consider when selecting the right printer for your marketing pieces. Use the following points as your guide.

- **Specialization.** What kind of printing do the printers specialize in, based on the equipment they have, the average quantities they run, their typical customer base, their business mission, and the level of quality they produce? In particular, find out if they specialize in 2-color or 4-color offset, digital, book, gang printing, or in POD (print on demand). Learning about their specialties will help you narrow your choice of printers quickly, and get you the best product for your budget.

- **Customer Support.** Does your sales representative respond to your requests promptly and thoroughly? Will you be assigned a production manager to help you with pre-press questions? Ask for the printer's references and call them.

- **Price.** Be sure to compare "apples to apples" when obtaining print bids. Use the exact same job specifications (i.e., paper, number of pages, size, etc.) when requesting a quote. Does the price include scans, proofs, pre-press set up, delivery costs, or shrink wrapping? Sometimes these items are included in the cost, and sometimes they are broken out.

- **Reliability.** Does the printer have a good reputation for meeting deadlines and shipping on time?

- **Quality.** Look at samples they have printed for other clients. Are they high quality? Are the pages trimmed evenly? Are there any smears, smudges? Do the colors match their proofs?

- **Electronic File Formats.** Will your printer accept files from your computer programs? More and more printers are accepting PDF files. If you plan to submit a PDF file, be sure to ask for a special "job options" file that includes the printer's PDF settings and file specifications.

- **Scheduling and Turnaround.** How long will the job take and when can it fit into the schedule? If the printer contracts with outside services to do part of the manufacturing (for example, binding services), it may add several days to the job.

- **Terms.** Does the printer require a deposit, the entire payment up front, or COD? Does it offer a payment plan or 30 days net? Be sure to ask. Most printers require a 50% deposit, a credit card, or a completed credit application.

What's the Difference Between a Digital and Offset Printer?

"Digital printing" can be a confusing term because the word "digital" is often used in different ways.

To clarify its use when printing your marketing materials, let me point out the differences between using a traditional offset press, a direct imaging offset press, and a digital printer. Take special note of the pricing examples below to help demystify beliefs about digital printing. Then decide for yourself which option is most cost-effective for your projects.

Traditional Offset Presses

Traditional offset printing uses a plate for each color on the press. Today, most plates are imaged from computer files, but in the past, they were made from film negatives or camera-ready artwork that was photographed using a large graphics camera.

The process of having a plate for each color is called color separation. Colors can be spot colors (found in the well-known PMS swatch book) or process colors (derived from a combination of cyan, magenta, yellow, and black inks, each having its own plate). If you want a wide spectrum of colors in your printed piece, you'd use process color.

Offset presses are generally more cost-effective than digital printers for long print runs (usually 1000 sheets or more). Printing only one color is the least expensive option; 2-color printing costs more than 1-color; 3-color printing costs more than 2-color, and so on.

With offset printing, you will incur set-up charges, including color proofs, plates, and "make-ready" pages. (Make-ready pages are the sheets of paper that first come off the press while it's getting warmed up. From examining make-ready pages, the press operator can adjust the flow of separate colored inks and achieve the desired balance of color.)

Answers To Your Printing Questions

Computer to Plate (CTP) Technology

Many printing companies now skip the step of producing negatives and go "direct to plate" by taking the computer file and imaging the plates on a platesetter. With this process, there's no need to make negatives. This technology is referred to as "computer-to-plate" or CTP.

Direct Imaging Presses (Digital Offset)

Some newer offset presses are equipped to image plates on the press, and these include the Heidelberg DI, Adast DI and Presstek DI. These presses are a good fit for jobs between 500 and 5,000 sheets.

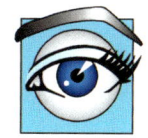

Eye-Popping Tip: *A typical sheet size is 11" x 17", therefore you can print two 8.5" x 11" flyers on one sheet, doubling the quantity.*

Full-Color Digital Printers

Digital printing equipment such as the Xerox DocuColor or HP Indigo do *not* require printing plates. Because these presses do not use make-readies, negatives, or plates, they are the most cost-effective option for short runs (usually less than 500 sheets per job).

Digital printers can also print variable data (for example, addresses from a postcard mailing list or consecutive numbers on gift certificates). Also, because they only print either CMYK or black ink, costs are generally the same whether you print one color or four colors.

Price Comparison Chart

Project: 8.5" x 11" flyer on 100-pound glossy text paper printed on one side, 1000 copies, with the following specifications:

4-color on Digital Printer......................................$300–$375
1-color on Offset Press (Traditional or CTP)........$200–$250
2-color on Offset Press (Traditional or CTP)........$275–$325
3-color on Offset Press (Traditional or CTP)........$375–$425
4-color on Offset Press (Traditional or CTP)........$600–$800
4-color on Offset Press (Gang Printer)*................$300–$375

* *See the following page for a definition of "gang printer."*

Please note: This is a general chart of prices for comparison purposes only. Your printing company's prices may be higher or lower, depending on many factors including turnaround time.

How Can You Save Money on Color Printing?

New technological advances in computer software and printing equipment have lowered the cost of printing on certain jobs but you're faced with high-cost decisions on whether to use 4-color printing or not. Here are a few suggestions you might try.

1. **If you need a short full-color run** (usually less than 500 sheets), find a printer who offers digital color printing. By using this process, you don't pay for negatives, make-readies, or plates, and you can print variable data (for example, addresses on post cards). The Xerox DocuColor is a toner-based digital color press and the HP Indigo is an ink-based digital color press.

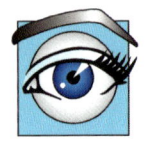

Eye-Popping Tip: *The quality of digital printing has improved to the point that sometimes it is difficult to distinguish digitally-printed pieces from traditional offset printing.*

2. **Find a printing company that does "gang" printing.** This printer usually specializes in certain types of 4-color process jobs, such as business cards, postcards, or 8.5" x 11" flyers. They can offer cost savings to customers by printing multiple jobs on one large press at the same time. Each customer shares the expensive 4-color "set-up" costs with all the others on the same job, so everyone's price goes down. The disadvantage is that your turnaround time is affected if you have to wait for the other orders to arrive. You also lose the opportunity to choose the paper you want—all jobs are printed on the same large sheet, then cut apart. Similarly, you lose customized control over your job. For example, you cannot ask the printer to adjust the colors on the press to your specifications. Sometimes unexpected color shifts will occur on your printed piece.

3. **Pre-print color "shells" of common, repeating elements.** If you have a newsletter, promotional campaign, or other multiple issue publication, you'll then use these shells for several issues. On the shell, you would design a newsletter with your logo, masthead, and tag line in color. Print these elements, leaving white space for the custom information that will appear in each

issue. Have your printer do enough shells for a one-year cycle, then store them and pull from them for each issue. New information gets printed on the shell in black ink. With this option, you only have to pay for color printing once.

5. **Use full-color pre-printed papers.** This option is recommended only for very short runs on a shoestring budget. It requires weighing the cost savings against the loss of customization and possible loss of quality for your printed piece. These papers come in a variety of designs for all occasions and in layouts for business cards, trifold brochures, flyers, letterheads, reply-cards, and more. In many cases, matching presentation folders, greeting cards, and thank you notes are also available. The papers have a graphic "theme" in a frame around each panel, with the center area open for you to add your content. You purchase these papers in packages of 25 to 50 sheets and design your content to fit into the open areas. Put the pre-printed papers in your black and white laser printer or ink jet printer and print the content in black. A few disadvantages come with this option. You won't be able to edit or move the color graphics because they're already printed. The business cards are perforated and may be printed on paper that isn't as thick as you might like. Be aware that perforated business cards may look "cheap" and the pre-printed designs may look familiar because they come from artwork that is "stock" and not original to you.

How Can You Maximize Two-Color Printing?

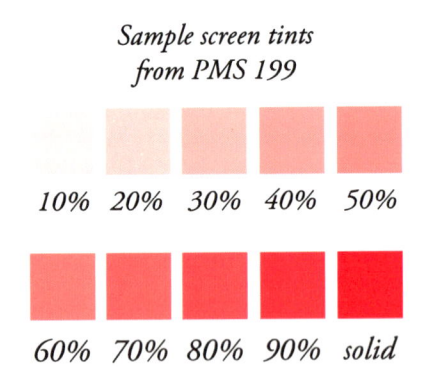

Sample screen tints from PMS 199

10% 20% 30% 40% 50%

60% 70% 80% 90% solid

Sometimes you will want more than just a black and white (B&W) document. Printing in two colors is an economical way to add additional color and pizzazz. Black and a second color are often used on stationery items and newsletters. PMS (Pantone Matching System), and TOYO are the most common inks used in "spot color" printing. You can pick from hundreds of custom-mixed colors.

In a layout with one predominately used color, a second color will emphasize important parts of your layout. Remember, just a small amount of strategically placed contrasting color will draw the eye to a focal point.

Spot color inks can be tinted (screened) from 5 percent to 100% (solid). (See samples on the left). Using screens adds variety to your layout and the illusion of more colors. Screens can be applied to text and graphics, or as rectangles behind certain areas to help organize or separate parts of the page.

A section of the PMS ink swatch book

Answers To Your Printing Questions

"Duotones" are made by printing a photo in two different inks. Shown on the left are a black and white photo and a duotone made from PMS 159 (orange) and black inks. Specific duotone color combinations can evoke certain feelings or moods. Notice how the orange and black duotone adds warmth to the portrait.

Printing spot colors will incur press "wash-up" charges, usually between $18 and $25 per ink. Print all your stationery items at the same time to save on multiple wash-up charges and to maintain consistent color. Because of the way different press operators mix the ink and distribute it on the rollers, sometimes you will see slight color shifts. Request a "press check" to see your job as it begins to print.

Original B&W Photo

A duotone photo made with PMS 159 and black ink creates a warmer photo than a standard black and white photo.

Black and PMS 159

The invitation on the left is made with only two spot colors: Black and PMS 312

Text is 20% screen tint of PMS 312

Rectangle is solid PMS 312

Duotone photo is Black & PMS 312

The duotones on this page are for simulation purposes only.

119

What Paper Works Best?

Choosing the right paper affects the success or failure of your book, direct mail piece, annual report, stationery, brochure, or package design. This summary will help you make the right decision about what kind of paper to use for your printed marketing pieces.

Defining Papers by Grade

Grade refers to a category of paper, based on the paper's primary use. It also represents a quality rating, from premium (the best), to #1, #2, #3, etc. By category, there are five basic grades of paper: bond, offset or uncoated book, coated book, text, and cover. Within each grade are other characteristics: brightness, opacity, bulk, color, finish, and fiber content.

Defining Paper by Basis Weight

Paper is also identified by basis weight. Basis weight is the weight of 500 "standard size" sheets of paper cut into a basis size. However, standard size sheets vary in size from grade to grade. Two similar sheets of various grades may have different basis weights. In addition, coated papers are compressed, so they may weigh more, but don't feel any thicker. Bond paper usually comes in 16# for forms, 20# for copying, and 24# for stationery. Offset ranges in weight from 50# to 70#. Coated book generally comes in 30# to 70# for web presses, and 60# to 110# for sheetfed. Text paper ranges from 60# to 100#. Cover paper usually comes in 60# to 100#, with duplex cover stocks doubling these numbers.

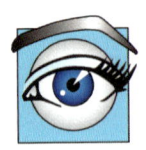

Eye-Popping Tip: *It is best to obtain a free swatch book from your paper representative before purchasing or specifying paper for your printer or designer. The swatch book will give you the opportunity to examine and feel the various sheets for finish, thickness, stiffness, opacity (translucence), and color.*

Grade	Common Names	Characteristics	Common Uses
Bond	bond, copier, erasable ledger, rag, writing	light weight, matching envelopes, pastels, watermarked	certificates, flyers, forms, letterheads, newsletters, resumes, lasers, copiers
Offset or Uncoated Book	book, offset, opaque	easy folding, smooth, wide range of colors	books, brochures, calendars, catalogs, direct mail, flyers, manuals, newsletters
Coated Book	coated offset, dull, enamel, gloss, matte, slick	good ink holdout, ink gloss, smooth surfaces, usually white only, yields vivid colors and excellent photo reproduction	annual reports, books, brochures, calendars, catalogs, direct mail, magazines, newsletters, newspaper inserts, posters
Text	text	textured, wide range of colors	annual reports, announcements, art reproductions, books, brochures, calendars, posters, self-mailers
Cover	bristol, C1S, C2S, cast-coated, cover, text cover	durable, stiff, strong, available in coated or uncoated, available in duplex (2 different color sheets laminated together)	business cards, calendars, folders, greeting cards, invitations, menus, point of purchase displays, postcards, posters, covers for annual reports, books, and catalogs

Adapted from "Step-By-Step Graphics: Designer's Guide to Paper," © *1987 by Dynamic Graphics, Inc.*

Brightness

Brightness is the amount of light that the paper reflects. Brighter paper will reflect more light through a printed photograph, resulting in photos that pop off the page. Type also will be more legible on brighter paper, but a very bright paper may cause too much eyestrain in long documents (e.g., book interiors).

Visual and Printed Opacity

Visual opacity is the light-blocking properties of the paper. Hold a sheet of paper up to the light and see how much shows through. Opacity is measured as a contrast ratio. The opacity of the majority of printing papers is 80 percent to 98 percent. It increases with bulk, coating, uneven surfaces, and the use of pigments (color), fillers, and ground wood. A sheet that is more opaque makes the text more readable and causes less eyestrain. Printed opacity is how much of the ink from one side soaks through the paper. Both of these characteristics are important considerations for two-sided and folded pieces.

Bulk

Bulk describes the thickness of the paper and is defined as pages per inch, or PPI. You will need to calculate the thickness of the finished piece to design the width of the spine or binding. If you have a thin book and want a wider spine, consider using a paper with more bulk.

Color

Papers come in an enormous array of hues. Even among white paper, there is a range from cooler, blue-grey whites to warmer, creamy whites. Remember, ink is translucent so the paper color will affect the resulting ink color. Warm paper will make colors look warmer. Color photos printed on a pure white paper will result in a closer match to your original color prints.

Finish

Finish is the texture of the paper's surface. Paper can be as smooth as chrome or as rough as particle board. Cast-coated, premium, ultra gloss and gloss finish are the shiniest finishes, generally found on coated stock. These papers have a layer of clay and other chemicals that form a smooth veneer on top of the paper.

Coated paper does not necessarily mean gloss, since a coated paper can also have a matte or dull finish. Uncoated papers can vary from the smoothest finish (machine finish) to a slightly toothy finish (vellum, antique, and eggshell) to the embossed finishes (felt, linen, laid, ribbed, and lined finish).

Eye-Popping Tip: *If you need to write on the actual printed piece (i.e., business reply cards or forms), do not select a gloss finish because the ink from a ballpoint pen will smear when used on that surface.*

The more textured a paper, the more ink will soak in, causing colors and halftones (photos) to become muted and/or muddy. Special steps are taken by the designer or pre-press department to adjust for ink holdout.

In bright lighting conditions, readability is easier on a matte finish rather than a gloss finish because there is less glare coming off the paper.

Recycled Papers

Recycled papers are virtually indistinguishable from their non-recycled counterparts, with similar performance, color, cost, and availability. Recycled paper varies on the percent of post-consumer waste (recycled fiber). Contact your paper rep for specific information on recycled paper. You will find the recycled paper symbol on any recycled paper regardless of post-consumer material content.

What Special Effects Will Add Flair to Your Print Job?

You may want to consider using one of these unique processes to add pizzazz to a special job. They are implemented during the "finishing" stage, and will add to the cost of your piece. Ideal jobs for these special effects are pocket folders, brochures, and invitations.

Embossing

Embossing uses a metal die, heat, and pressure to reshape the surface of paper. Embossing raises the image above the paper surface while debossing lowers the image. Unless combined with foils (described below), it is referred to as "blind embossing." A small magnesium die (for example, a logo on your business card) may cost $100. You will need a more expensive brass die for intricate designs, beveled edges, sculptured images, or for print runs longer than 1000 impressions. Dies are priced on size, intricacy, and material—brass being the best quality. Embossing is very attractive on textured cover-weight papers (for example, pocket folders).

Foil Stamping (or Foiling)

Foil stamping is a process that uses a heated die to stamp and adhere a special mylar-backed material to paper. Foils come in many colors and materials (including metallic and pearlescence), special patterns, and designs. You can combine foil stamping with embossing to create a more striking 3D image.

Diecuts

Diecuts are areas that are completely or partially punched out with a steel blade (like a cookie cutter). A diecut can be as simple as a slit designed to hold the corners of a business card to a folder. Die cuts on the outside of a piece allow part of an interior image to show through on the outside. These effects can be quite creative. Your entire piece may be diecut into a unique shape!

Some common uses of diecuts are rounded corners, door hanger slits, flaps, holes, windows, and pop-ups. Many printers keep a number of these common dies in stock.

A pictorial example of embossing

Varnish

Varnish is a liquid shellac put on a printed piece to add a glossy, satin, or dull finish. It is applied like a final layer of ink after your piece is printed. It may be clear or tinted. Varnish can be used to reduce glare or enhance readability. Spot gloss varnish applied to photos printed on a coated, matte paper will make the photos "pop." Aqueous coating is a more durable process that provides protection from fingerprints, scuffing, and scratches. UV-coating provides a high-gloss, rubbery, clear finish.

Curl-free Laminate

This is a film laminate that is used mostly on paperback book covers to add protection and durability. It comes in a gloss or matte finish.

Fifth Color

You may notice that certain PMS colors do not reproduce well when printed with 4-color process (CMYK) inks. If your logo is one of these PMS colors, you may consider running a "fifth color." In addition to the 4-color process inks, the printer would add the same PMS color ink that you normally use on your spot color jobs (for example, your stationery package) as your fifth color. The PMS ink would make your logo color match the color of your logo on your stationery materials.

What Kind of Folding Do You Need?

Double Parallel Fold

Gate Fold

Roll or Barrel Fold

French Fold

Accordion Fold

Single Fold

Letter Fold

There are many ways to fold paper . . . think of the art of origami! When designing your marketing pieces, you may consider using a fold or two in your brochure or flyer.

You probably are most familiar with the single fold and letter fold. A letter fold is sometimes referred to as a "trifold" because there are three panels per side. Other common folds in the production industry are: double parallel fold, gate fold, roll fold, french fold, and accordion fold.

Folding is done during the "binding and finishing" stage of production. The procedure will be priced according to the complexity of the fold. As you can see, there are some complex folds illustrated here. Because folding is a somewhat imprecise procedure, leave room for variations in the folds. Each fold is affected by the variation in the previous fold as well.

Paper stock also affects the fold. Heavier weight paper such as cover stock and thicker text stock will require a "score" first before the fold. A score makes an impression like a crease in the paper where the fold will be. With the score, when the paper is folded, the ridge of the folded paper will be smooth. Without the score, the paper will crack and feel bumpy along the ridge. Heavy ink coverage over the fold and coated papers should also be scored to prevent cracking.

The paper should be folded along the "grain." The grain is the general direction of most of the fibers in the paper. Your printer will advise you how the paper was cut so you can be sure that it will be folded along the grain.

When laying out the panels, remember that the inner panels will be a bit shorter in width than the outside panels. This allows the paper to bend around the fold and meet up with the other edge. Be sure to use the type of fold that is appropriate for your piece. Lay it out so that the flow of information is correct for the natural opening process. Remember that the post office prefers the fold to be along the bottom on the mailing panel.

What are Your Options for Binding?

Just as you have many choices for printers, paper, and folding, you'll find lots of options for binding your projects, too. Each binding method has a specific benefit, whether it's low cost, durability, or the ability to lie flat when open. Be sure to ask your printer for advice on choosing the appropriate binding for your project.

Here are some of the most common binding methods and applications for each of them.

Case Bound (Hard Cover)

You would likely choose this kind of binding for reference books, archival materials, textbooks, children's books, and gift books.

With case bound binding, the signatures of paper (usually one signature is 32 pages) are glued together, then glued to a gauze strip. After that, the entire book block is glued with end sheets onto hard covers. For added durability, the signatures can be sewn together first, allowing the book to lie flatter than a perfect bound book (see on the next page) but not as flat as Wire-O® or spiral bound books (see on the following pages). The spine of the book can be squared or rounded depending on the equipment that the case binder has. Notice it has hinges (grooves) along the edges of the cover near the spine.

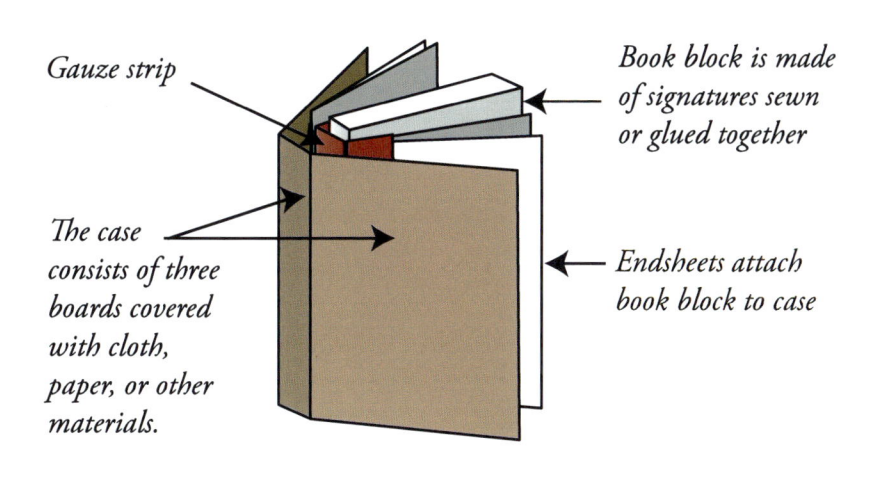

Gauze strip

The case consists of three boards covered with cloth, paper, or other materials.

Book block is made of signatures sewn or glued together

Endsheets attach book block to case

Some hard covers feature printed artwork laminated to the boards. Others can have dust covers, which are the paper "jackets" you see on books. Those books with dust covers usually have a cloth covering on the boards. Alternatively, they could have paper covers that look like cloth, but are less expensive. The title of the book may be foil stamped onto the spine and/or front cover.

Signatures are hot glued to spine.

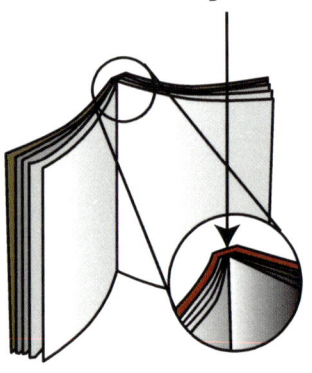

Perfect Bound (Soft Cover)

Most commonly used for paperback books and documents, soft covers are bound in a similar way as hard cover books. Perfect binding is also used to bind novels, annual reports, and self-help books.

With this type, after the signatures are gathered, the spine is ground to create a rough surface and then glued to a paper cover. For added durability, the spine can be notched (cut with v-shaped slits), allowing more surface for glue. This is called notch-perfect binding. While the glue is still hot, the paper cover gets wrapped around the spine. Alternatively, you can ask to have the signatures sewn instead of glued. The sewn option allows the book to open somewhat flat, though not as much as other kinds of bindings.

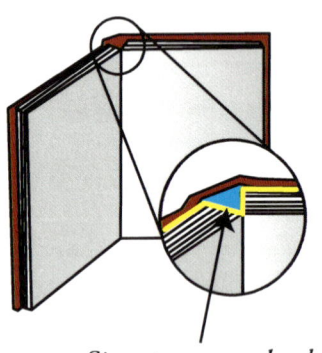

Otabind or Lay Flat

Otabind or Lay Flat binding is frequently used for technical manuals, directories, cookbooks, and reference books. In this type of binding, the signatures are gathered and glue is applied to the spine, then the book block is capped covering only the glue. The capping is side glued and a cover is applied, adhering only to the side glue and detached from the spine. This particular process was patented, but the patent has expired, which is why you'll hear the term "Lay Flat" binding more often than Otabind.

Its advantage is in its name; a book with Lay Flat binding opens completely. You'll find it's much easier to use a cookbook that lies flat on a counter than one you have to hold in your hands to read.

Signatures are glued to a cloth, which floats above the spine board.

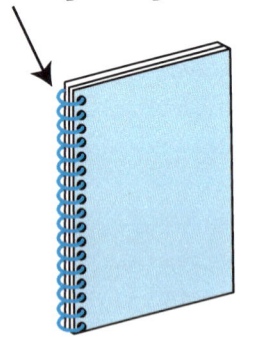

Spiral Bound

You'll find that spiral binding is well suited for short prints runs of reports, brochures, presentation materials, workbooks, and manuals.

With this type of binding, the cover and interior pages are punched with holes through which a single plastic or wire spiral is inserted. You'll find the plastic spirals available in many colors and wire spirals mostly available in black. This versatile, inexpensive binding allows the pages to lie flat, although they may not align exactly. Beware: The ends of the spiral can snag fabric and other things.

Single metal wire or colored plastic spiral

Answers To Your Printing Questions

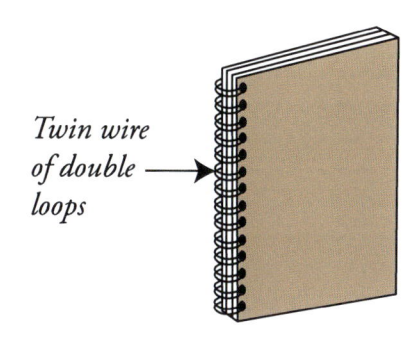

Twin wire of double loops

Wire-O® Binding

Used for reference manuals, address books, cookbooks, and journals, this type of versatile, durable binding will allow the pages to lie perfectly flat on a counter or table.

With this type, the cover and interior pages are punched with holes through which a double looped wire is inserted. Why a double looped wire? Because it allows for nearly perfect alignment between pages. Ask your designer or printer for additional variations available.

Saddle Stitched

Used on thin booklets, brochures, newsletters, and catalogs, saddle stitching is among the most widely used and inexpensive kinds of binding available.

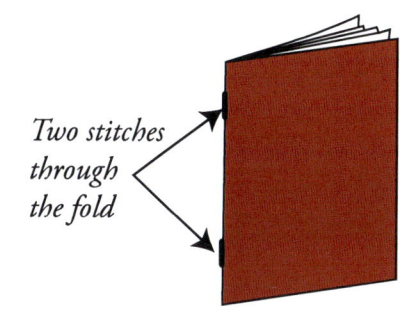

Two stitches through the fold

With this type of binding, the signatures are all gathered and folded together. Then they are placed over a "saddle" and stapled along the spine. The book lies relatively flat, but it doesn't have a spine and may not last under heavy use. Quick to assemble, saddle stitching can accommodate gate folds and foldouts.

If your document is thicker than a quarter of an inch, you likely won't be able to use this style of binding.

Side Stitched

Also a fast, easy, and inexpensive type of binding, side stitching requires a minimum of a one-inch margin on the spine side. It's commonly used for digitally produced documents, manuals, and large brochures.

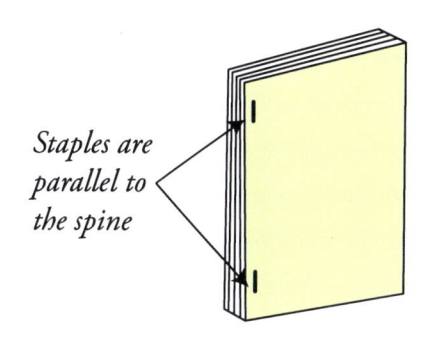

Staples are parallel to the spine

With this type of binding, the loose pages and cover are stitched together with staples on the outside of the book block. The cover can be two sheets or one sheet wrapped around the spine. It won't allow the pages to lie flat and thickness of the document is limited.

From these choices, it becomes clear that various applications call for different kinds of bindings. Ask your printer for the kind best recommended for your project.

Resources

Many thanks to Dick Bruso, Barbara McNichol, Kendall Summer-Hawk, Joyce Turley, and Julie Wassom, for their contributions to this guide. This fine group of professionals have years of invaluable wisdom and experience in their fields. If you would like to use their services, be sure to let them know you found them in this guide.

Dick Bruso

An accomplished speaker, author, and branding expert, Dick Bruso is the founder of Heard Above The Noise™, a highly regarded and nationally recognized branding firm. As a creative branding consultant, Dick helps create and implement powerful branding, marketing, media, and relationship-building strategies to position his clients to be "heard above the noise" in the marketplace. He can be reached at 303-841-5122 or via email at dickbruso@heardabove.com. His website address is www.heardabove.com

Barbara McNichol—Editor

Authors, speakers, and entrepreneurs turn to writer/editor Barbara McNichol to perfect their books, articles, and marketing materials. To sign up for her free monthly e-zine "The Door Opener," call 877-696-4899, email: editor@barbaramcnichol.com or visit www.BarbaraMcNichol.com

Kendall SummerHawk—Website and Marketing Consultant

Kendall SummerHawk is a leading self-employment expert, author of the book *Brilliance Unbridled,* and popular speaker. Kendall's client-capturing Website Wisdom package and her unique Brilliance Unbridled marketing program help self-employed professionals step up to the next level of passionate, profitable business success. Visit her site at www.KendallSummerHawk.com or call 520-577-6404.

Joyce M. Turley—Illustrator

Illustrating books on all topics for readers of all ages, Joyce Turley provides custom artwork to enhance your printed and digital media. Line art to full-color paintings, picture books to technical renderings, interiors and book covers. Visit www.dixoncovedesign.com or call 970-226-2461.

Julie Wassom—Marketing Trainer and Consultant

Julie Wassom, president of The Julian Group, Inc., is a speaker, consultant, and author specializing in helping businesses drive revenue and increase profitability through marketing and sales. She is the author of *The Marketing and Sales Success Library* and the free e-zine "Wassom's Marketing Wisdom." Julie can be reached at 303-693-2306 or by email at julie@juliewassom.com. Her website is www.juliewassom.com

What Comes Next...

You've followed the path to creating eye-catching graphics and stepped up your marketing—just from applying the ideas and techniques in *Turn Eye Appeal into Buy Appeal*. In the process, you have:

- determined the purpose of your project
- identified your intended target audience
- decided on what graphic information to include
- developed your branding, including a graphics theme
- referred to your design standards manual (or created one)
- created an image in your mind of your final product
- made decisions how to produce it start to finish
- talked with your printer about print specifications
- prepared your print-ready files properly
- researched needed postal regulations
- set your schedule of activities and lined up assistance
- assigned a cost for each step of the process
- and much more!

Congratulations—you've accomplished a lot! And if you haven't followed this process exactly but skipped around, I hope you've found quick solutions to your immediate design problems. That's what I've designed this guide to do—to make your design life easier and your marketing pieces shine!

What Else Can This Guide Can Do For You?

In a light, conversational style that won't bog you down in technical terms, *Turn Eye Appeal into Buy Appeal* addresses these common scenarios and more:

- how to make visual elements a critical part of your branding strategy
- how to "hook" customers with persuasive words and writing
- how to make your fonts match your message well
- how to jazz up your layouts with grids, pull quotes, and more
- how to apply specific design solutions to flyers, websites, presentations, and manuscripts
- how to work with digital photography
- how to use color to add "zing" to your marketing pieces
- how to prepare design files differently for the Internet versus the printer
- how to communicate with a printer so you can prepare your files correctly
- and so much more!

I'm Happy to Share Information and Resources

If you need assistance or resources in creating your marketing pieces, I encourage you to visit my website at **www.macgraphics.net.** And if you haven't done so already, sign up for my free monthly ezine "Graphics Image Builder." In fact, I based the content of this guide on several years of producing this ezine. By subscribing, you'll add even more knowledge to what you've gained from using *Turn Eye Appeal into Buy Appeal.*

Of course (do I even need to say this?) feel free to email me personally at **Karen@macgraphics.net** or call me toll-free at **888-796-7300**. I'd love to hear your success stories—the small ideas that have made BIG differences in your marketing. And share your best Eye-Popping Tips, too!

To your marketing success,

Karen Saunders

Karen Saunders

CPSIA information can be obtained
at www.ICGtesting.com
Printed in the USA
2713LVUK00006B